Flannery O'Connor's South

ROBERT COLES

FLANNERY O'CONNOR'S SOUTH

BROWN THRASHER BOOKS
The University of Georgia Press
Athens and London

Published in 1993 as a Brown Thrasher Book
by the University of Georgia Press, Athens, Georgia 30602

The paper in this book meets the guidelines
for permanence and durability of the Committee on
Production Guidelines for Book Longevity
of the Council on Library Resources.

Printed in the United States of America

05 04 03 02 01 P 7 6 5 4 3

Library of Congress Cataloging in Publication Data

Coles, Robert.
Flannery O'Connor's South / Robert Coles
p cm
"Brown thrasher books "
Originally published: Baton Rouge . Louisiana State University
Press, 1980
Includes bibliographical references
ISBN 0-8203-1536-2 (pbk · alk paper)
1 O'Connor, Flannery—Homes and haunts—Southern States.
2. Authors, American—20th century—Biography. 3 Southern States—
Intellectual life—1865- 4 Southern States in literature.
I. Title
PS3565 C57Z63 1993
813' 54—dc20 92-41956
[B] CIP

British Library Cataloging in Publication Data available

To Richard Poirier
To David Riesman

CONTENTS

And when I saw Him, I fell at His feet as dead. And He laid his right hand upon me, saying unto me "Fear not, I am the first and the last."

I am He that liveth and was dead; and behold, I am alive evermore Amen; and I have the keys of hell and of death.

Write the things which thou hast seen, and the things which are, and the things which shall be hereafter.

THE REVELATIONS OF ST. JOHN THE DIVINE
I, 17–19

PREFACE TO THE BROWN THRASHER EDITION

FOR MORE THAN THIRTY YEARS NOW, my wife, Jane (a high school English teacher), and I have been keeping company with Flannery O'Connor's fictional characters—not to mention the author herself—as she is revealed to us through her essays (collected as *Mystery and Manners*) and her letters (collected as *The Habit of Being*). Each year at Harvard, I bring her voice and vision, her wonderfully drawn characters to the attention of my students (medical students and undergraduate students, and yes, business students), and quickly we are responding to the provocative ironies and the edifying paradoxes she poses for her readers. As one medical student told me, "You're not quite the same after you've finished with her." He stopped and took note of the way he had just spoken: he had left out the penultimate word "reading" and in so doing, he had spoken rather more suggestively than he had perhaps intended. Then he decided to be playful with what he had said, with what he would say: "Actually, I could put it this way—you're not quite the same after she's finished with you!"

I thought at the time, and still do, that Flannery O'Connor would have loved that remark. She had such an eye for human complexity; she could fit that complexity nevertheless into the plain, ordinary, blunt idiom of everyday life. Moreover, she was unashamedly assertive, if not truculent, in certain important respects. And yes, she did want us all to be done with a lot of peculiar nonsense that has been touted in this century as a kind of breakthrough knowledge, even wisdom. She also wanted to make clear her impatience, her annoyance even, with those of us who are eternally gullible, or so it seems, ready to worship new idols even before the old ones have lost their grip on us. So that medical student was right to more than hint at the powerfully insistent side of O'Connor's voice which was a determination, I often think, to grab ahold ("aholt"!) of us late twentieth-century readers, and give us more than a run for our money. It was her hope, I suspect, that a lot of us would be "finished" after meeting up with, say, Sheppard of "The Lame Shall Enter First," or Mr. Head of "The Artificial Nigger," or Julian of "Everything That Rises Must Converge," or Hulga of "Good Country People." They are all the same person, and Miss O'Connor would be the first to remind us that she had met that person in the mirror, even as she hoped we'd be lucky enough to catch more than a glimpse of ourselves through whatever self-reflection those relentlessly incisive stories might prompt in us.

All the time she dared to evoke the sinful, self-important pride of us secular folk who are so sure of what we know, so pleased with all the "progress" we've made, that we overlook what is still, alas, a big part of ourselves—the capacity to be blinded by self-absorption, hence all too unknowingly hurtful of others, who don't exist for us as others, but rather as foils for our various wishes and needs. Brilliant, well-educated minds can embrace Nazi hate, and humble people, with no claim to moral virtue, can be decent and honorable in ways that are admirable almost beyond words: those who risked their lives to save men, women, and children hunted by the Gestapo in 1930s and 1940s Europe, or those in Flannery O'Connor's native South who dared to take on the segregationist principalities and powers. She, of course, worried that in the name of such important and much-needed efforts for social change in her beloved region, plenty of arrogance and callousness would be let loose. Alas, her concerns were not proved totally groundless. Still, it would be a mistake to connect her fictional themes to specific political or racial struggles. She kept her eyes fastened on that larger scene—on us fallen creatures whose moral and spiritual life is in more jeopardy than we seem to realize. She was, put differently, a writer of biblical sensibility, anxious to explore matters good and evil with a keen sense of our human vulnerability and frailty.

It is something of a miracle then (and also an irony) that this storyteller (who, in certain respects, is kin spiritually to the Hebrew prophets, not to mention a member of the Catholic church's saints) has continued to elicit such strong interest from many who might not at all object to being described as members of the liberal intelligentsia. As a matter of fact, I am surprised, even stunned, at the response given to her work by students who have never gone to church or to a synagogue, or are "agnostic." And yet they are stirred (often anxiously, even apprehensively) to reflection, as they ponder, for example, what happens in "The Displaced Person" or "The Enduring Chill." But my surprise tells of a lapse on my part—a forgetfulness with respect to the lacerating power a storyteller can possess. Last spring a student told us all in a literature and ethics seminar I teach at the Harvard Business School what had happened to her as she went through "The Displaced Person," and then sat back to try to make sense of it. "At first I wondered why you'd assigned that story to us. It seemed to be about events in a small southern farming community, and the people seemed weird to me—I mean, I couldn't figure them out, and they weren't like people I know. But by the time I was through reading [it], I realized that I *did* know what was going on: greed was at work, and an insensitivity to others, to everyone but herself [on the part of Mrs. McIntyre]. She's the one who became the 'displaced person' in the end—when I saw that, when I realized it, I was hit hard. I thought to myself, I asked, 'Will you end up being like that?'"

No great eloquence from a young woman approaching thirty, who had done well, already, on Wall Street after attending Yale as a major in economics. She grew up in a fancy town outside of Philadelphia and hardly qualifies as the reader who is apt to grasp every subtlety and nuance of O'Connor's writing. Yet she had most certainly figured out a good deal of what the author intended her readers to begin considering.

This book is not meant, of course, to supply a series of interpretations of the above-mentioned stories, or of others, or of O'Connor's two novels. Nor do I intend to say that the characters O'Connor *imagined*—those extraordinarily compelling people who populate her fiction—are to be confused with all sorts of "real" people (for instance, the various kinds of southerners who live in or near Milledgeville or elsewhere in the South). In no way does Miss O'Connor need someone running ahead of her, or behind her, putting the imprimatur of social factuality on her various creations. They stand quite solidly on their own. On the other hand, I don't think she'd mind the observation that her stories draw on a particular social, cultural, and religious world (she has said so several times). And I don't think she'd mind a response to her stories that isn't that of the literary critic (she could be fairly sardonic, actually, toward some of the reviews and interpretations of her work that came to her attention), but rather that of an itinerant Yankee observer who happened to put in over a decade in the South and who lived in Georgia for four years in a town of about two hundred souls—some of which, I used to think, were close kin to those O'Connor sent our way from Milledgeville.

Even in the early 1960s, before she died in August in 1964, O'Connor's idiosyncratic moral imagination had worked its way into the lives of many of us; so much so that, at the Westminster School in Atlanta, where my wife taught an English class, a janitor who was given to mumbling pieties, shaking his head long and hard when he heard people fight each other with words, and praying on his knees now and then in the midst of his work, was promptly declared by many not a "psychiatric case" (or a medical one) but rather, "a Flannery O'Connor type." My wife always wanted clarification of course, and the young people she taught weren't usually off the mark. She had taught them O'Connor's stories, and the students had gotten familiar enough with a great writer's vision, close enough to the assumptions and apprehensions that inform a substantial and quite coherent body of work to make certain connections between what someone did that was "odd" in a rather privileged suburban private school (where that janitor was *sui generis*) and what O'Connor had some of her characters try to do: take life exceedingly seriously, much to the confusion and alarm of others.

I hope that this book will help a few readers understand people not rarely misunderstood. Some of those people, I think it fair to say, were Flannery O'Connor's teachers, and, in a way, she anointed them—dispatched them to those all too ready to look down their noses at various flaws in others while failing to glimpse a few of their own. As she knew to say, she had a continuing series of fish to fry. And the vivid colloquialisms and expressions, the dramatic turns of speech and thought and manner and outlook that are part and parcel of the lives of some of her fellow southerners still, helped her mightily, gave her the cooking oil, it might be said. As for the fish and the fire to cook them . . . well, all that was a gift of God, I'm fairly sure she would acknowledge that. And for us it is a most significant and enduring gift indeed—a gift for which many of us keep saying thanks in classrooms and elsewhere almost three decades after her untimely departure from this world. A departure that was in her mind a mere prelude, anyway, to another, far more important and lasting place of residence.

INTRODUCTION

MY WIFE AND I read and read again Flannery O'Connor's stories and her two novels when we were living and working in the South—Mississippi, Louisiana, Georgia—during the late 1950s and the first half of the 1960s. For several years we lived outside a small town, Vinings, northwest of Atlanta in Cobb County; and as we became acquainted with some of the people there, black and white, we found ourselves referring to one, then another O'Connor character or situation. In the first volume of *Women of Crisis* we made mention of a brief time we had with a writer we had come to admire enormously, and learn from constantly. "To see Georgia," we said, "or any part of the South, through Flannery O'Connor's eyes is to be reminded that any segment of human experience—described by words such as *race, sex, class*, or regional affiliation—ought in some way to be given its place in a larger scheme of things." We badly needed, at the time, that particular reminder. We were, ourselves, all caught up in studies of school desegregation, in the activities of the civil rights movement. Yankee outsiders (though first residents of Mississippi, in 1958, by military assignment, under the Doctors' Draft law) we were intent on moral indignation, political change, and, as the words went, "participant observation," one more phrase of the social sciences that lends itself, occasionally, to the purpose of self-importance and self-congratulation. I say "we," but I ought to have switched, in the sentence immediately above, to "I."

My wife is an English teacher, and in 1960, say, while I was reading all sorts of books on "the Negro" and "the South," she was turning the pages, yet again, of *Wise Blood* and the various stories that made up *A Good Man Is Hard To Find*. In a concluding section of our initial book on women, it was my wife who wrote, "Flannery O'Connor could take sociological matters such as 'segregation' and show them to be shadows created by the flames of hell." And, in a more personal vein: "We met and talked with her when we lived not too far from her. She was sick, dying. She spoke quite frankly of her illness and of her native South. She warned us not to become so caught up in a region's special (and then urgent) difficulties that we lost sight of what she referred to the several times we spoke, as 'the larger human drama in which all of us have our parts to play.'"

Then, in qualification and amplification: "She was not by any means trying to evade the specific challenges (and the outrages) of a particular 'way of life.' She knew in her heart how wretched and stunted various people could be in her native land. But her eyes scanned the sky in pursuit of God's judgment and also poked about various stretches of old clay in the sure knowledge that the Devil would be found at work in many guises. Her bitterly vivid portrayals of the evil creature in us are meant to shake from us a bit of the vanity and conceit that are, of course, inevitable companions of each human being—no matter the person's skin color, occupation, sex, religious creed."

And finally, returning to the autobiographical: "We found our talk with her unsettling, perplexing, distracting. There was so much to see and do in the South of the early 1960s; why get caught up in her exceedingly strenuous scruples and admonitions? Over the years, though, her words, her point of view, her advice have weighed heavier and heavier on our shoulders. 'You will find here in rural Georgia fallen angels by the thousands,' she told us, a twinkle in her eye, but only the thinnest of smiles on her hurt and saddened face. It was a nice way to give us one of those 'contexts' that get mentioned so often these days by social scientists, no great friends of hers."

We did not then feel it necessary to explain the rather peculiar circumstances under which, ever so briefly, we came to meet Flannery O'Connor. We were describing some of the women who had influenced our work; we were not trying to give still another account of that work. But it was, in fact, a black woman, who introduced us to a certain patient she was caring for: "She's a writer from down there in Baldwin

County." And we have often told one another, over the years, perhaps a bit presumptuously, that the writer to whom our friend Ruth Ann Jackson brought us might have enjoyed hearing how it came about that we all got together. Mrs. Jackson was the grandmother of one of the black students who pioneered Atlanta's school desegregation in 1961. We knew the granddaughter well. But we met the older woman first and rarely saw the youth without also spending time with Ruth Ann, as she insisted we call her: "I'm Ruth Ann, a lay minister of the Gospel. You're not going to call me Mrs. Jackson, and you're not going to call me Ruth. You can call me Reverend Ruth Ann, but that's too big a mouthful for you. Just spit out Ruth Ann, when you come around."

We'd been introduced to her about a half hour earlier. Yet there she was telling us in no uncertain terms what the gound rules were going to be. We had heard her do so a day before, rather more publicly. The city's school officials (nervously but with a self-assurance unmistakably white) had called in the parents of the black handful (ten out of thousands) chosen by a federal judge to begin the integration of a major southern urban school system. The blacks were asked to listen to a series of presentations—whites once more handing down the law. At the end the meeting was declared over. Out of fear of a riot, the people had come together in virtual secrecy, a hard fact to keep in mind these days, a mere fifteen or so years later, when Atlanta's mayor is black.

But one person was not going to allow things to end "as planned." Up stood an enormous woman, just under six feet in height, some 250 pounds on her frame. She was without apology and without apparent haste. She talked of her life—her life as the daughter of a sharecropper in the southeastern part of Georgia near Savannah, her life in Atlanta, her mental life, and, yes, her religious life. At the point that she sensed impatience, she became more assertive, anything but apologetic or plaintive: "You can all leave here as quick as you planned. But I want to tell you; I want to let you know. I want you never to forget—Him: Jesus Christ, Who made us all, and Who will judge us all. In the Bible we're told: 'I am He that liveth, and was dead; and behold I am alive for evermore, Amen; and have the keys of hell and of death.' I memorized that while in Milledgeville. I said it every day. Then, God gave me my mind back. Now I try to heal, like He did. I try to heal, working in the hospital. I try to heal my own children, and their children. I try to heal myself—the times when I want to kill someone who's looking down on me, who's on my back; who's forgotten that the Lord is our Father, and not Mammon, and not Caesar." She stopped with that piercing biblical allusion. Complete silence. A car's horn outside. A beginning, finally, of movement. The creak of chairs as they get pushed. But one more precise, urgently conveyed request: "Praise the Lord!"

As the people left, they took care to stay clear of her—blacks and whites alike. I did too. To be honest, I leaned toward my wife as we sat there—stunned, more than a little perplexed—and said some words; awful words, I now realize, and words that tell more about me than about Ruth Ann Jackson. My wife had to hear those words: "She's a disturbed woman." I heard neither an affirmation nor a disagreement. I went on, in my long-winded psychiatric best—or worst: "What an inappropriate thing to do, at such a moment. She expressed her anxieties; and she made everyone else anxious. She must have been in the state hospital for a while. Milledgeville is where it's located." My wife shook her head—I thought in puzzled, sad agreement. We made our way out of the room, down the elevator, into the rain-soaked street. Then came the brief, sharply worded rebuke: "Why don't you leave her alone! Why didn't you listen to her! Did you prefer the messages of those school bureaucrats?"

There was more, much more—the discussion of two "field workers." Or a tough confrontation—for each of us; in the words of a Georgia writer, "a late encounter with the enemy!" My wife was more than tired of my psychological reductionism, ever waiting for a suitable target—in this instance, supplied unashamedly by a woman's confessional mode of exclamation. I was unwilling to retract a word of my kind of (psychological, secular) judgment. Doctors may not have "the keys of hell and of death," but they do have their keys; doctors in Milledgeville, as a matter of fact. Let's stop romanticizing the South, black or white. Let's face down madness, wherever it is to be found. Let's get going with that "new South," a place that surely will be free of superstition, ignorance, illusions; free of what also may be called the grotesque, a word O'Connor had, on more than one occasion, found it necessary to contend with.

Eventually, we came to be frequent, sometimes daily, visitors of Ruth Ann Jackson's. She took care of her small grandchildren, while her daughter worked in a factory. Then, in the late afternoon, seemingly not tired, full of determination and energy, indeed ready to declare herself, Mrs. Jackson took herself to work, as a nurse's aide in an Atlanta hospital. She was glad to have that job, as she once explained to us: "My husband died five years ago. He had high blood pressure, and one day the Lord decided to call him home. It was early in the morning; I woke up, and there he was, moaning, and I asked what was wrong, and he didn't answer me, and I looked closer, and I knew it was real bad, real bad. I went to get him a cold wet cloth, and some tea, but when I came back, he was gone. I didn't cry. I thanked God. My husband had suffered a long time. He'd been poor all his life, but he had accepted Jesus Christ when I got out of the mental hospital. I'd told him: he could have me back, but only if he took Jesus Christ Almighty with me! He said yes, and I said yes, and it was like getting married again, only now there were the three of us.

"After he died, I didn't want to be at home in the evening. I was glad to help my daughter out with her kids, then go to work. That way, I'm so tired when I crawl into bed, I don't lie there, my eyes open, my head full of the devil, my toes going like mad, my hands all squeezed up; I just work myself under the blanket, and the next thing I know, I'm working myself out from the blanket, and setting my two feet on the floor again, and getting ready to say hello to God, and hello to a new day. I do that with a prayer: 'Thank you, Lord, for another look at this earth, and if You want me, I'll try to be ready, and I've sinned, but I believe, even if I disbelieve, and thank you again.' That's my prayer; no one taught it to me. I say it, and my head clears, and I'm ready to go again."

She loved hospital work. The better we got to know her, the more we heard about her life on those wards, in those various patients' rooms. She was a keen observer. She had a natural sense of the dramatic—the critical, revelatory moment in a particular chain of events. Her ears were sharp, were sensitively responsive to what was being spoken, and why. At times a preacher, a hectoring one at that, she could also be a silent, attentive listener. We were enthralled as we received a series of enactments—Ruth Ann telling us about this one and Ruth Ann mentioning someone else: nurses and doctors and patients, all white. And then there was the black side of a still segregated hospital: "We have our own place to change our clothes, and to eat; it's 'yes sir' and 'yes ma'am' country, that's what I call it. I leave the hospital, and I think of all I've tried to do, and the nice folks I've met, but I'm glad I don't have to yes the white people until the next day!"

She was telling us, around that time, how good it was for both us and her and others like her to talk about racial matters openly—to bring up annoyances and resentments and fears and worries. None of us could solve the larger (historical, social, political, economic) issues, but these were the personal ones, and, she never chose to forget, the religious ones—a matter of individuals and their faith, or lack of it. "The new Jerusalem begins with us, here in this room," she once insisted—a tenable theology, though I had trouble then, and still do, being quite so casual about what some social theorists call the structural problems of our South, of American society, of other countries as well. And there was talk of her "ministry," of her vocation, as a certain Atlanta preacher had told her to put it. She was sent here, she realized comparatively late in her life, to tell others of Christ. Her husband had been taken so that she could devote even more of her time to that purpose. Each day in the hospital she broached the subject of Jesus with her "colored friends." Sometimes there were opportunities with "the white ones." And what about us? Had we a vocation? If I was a doctor, then I ought to know about "Christian healing." If I was a writer, I had better remember Christ in what I was setting down in words. And speaking of writers, she told us one day, there was a writer in the hospital at that very time, and they'd been talking, and the writer "believed in God"—Ruth Ann knew that from what she'd seen and heard.

We had gone with Ruth Ann to the hospital a number of times. We knew one of the young doctors there, and we had visited two friends who had been operated upon there. But most of all, we knew her, and she wanted us to know her *there*. My wife began doing volunteer work, and had occasion to witness the force of this woman—her physical size more than matched by her willingness to be outspoken. She swaggered down corridors, her hips swaying, her thick arms going up and down, her mouth calling for blessings upon those of her co-workers she knew, and a few she didn't. She was a source of amusement to the white staff—a "funny character," one nurse called her. The hospital's blacks were made nervous by her—a mixture of awe, admiration, envy, perplexity. Where did she get the nerve to tell doctors that they looked tired, or that they weren't paying enough attention to one or another patient? "She's a sassy nigger," my wife heard a black woman say about Ruth Ann. "She's an uppity nigger, but she's fun," my wife heard a white woman, a nurse, say about Ruth Ann. And she obtained the attention of the patients, too—including a woman whom Ruth Ann kept calling "the writer." My wife didn't bother asking about "the writer" for a while; there had been others: "the lawyer," "the professor," "the store-owner," "the society lady," "the schoolteacher," "the secretary." But one day, in the hospital, Ruth Ann told my wife, who was pushing a cartful of books to room after room, that "stories" written by "the writer" should be purchased by the "hospital people" for the patients to read. And who is that "writer"? The answer: "Mizz Connor, Mizz *O'*Connor."

That is how "we," meaning my wife, came to meet "the writer"—under such strange and unfortunate circumstances. If my wife had any quibbles about entering Mizz O'Connor's room, she had to surrender them before the overwhelming moral authority of Ruth Ann, who told her that she must not "discriminate" against anyone who might want to read a book, "even a writer." Why that phrase? "Because writers may make books, but they need to read them, too," Ruth Ann explained. But I bring up Ruth Ann not only because it was through her that we had an ever so brief and restricted, but nonetheless memorable, acquaintance with an ailing but gracious Flannery O'Connor. A few weeks after "the writer" left the hospital for home, Ruth Ann left as well—and for reasons the author of "Everything That Rises Must Converge," or for that matter, "The River," or the novel *The Violent Bear It Away* might well have taken a decided interest in hearing told.

Ruth Ann had the misfortune, one working day, to hear a doctor speaking sharply to a patient—criticizing her for asking him too many questions. Later, at the ward station, and to the astonishment of the nurses and a scrubwoman nearby, Ruth Ann upbraided the man. She lost her job. But she had done the Lord's work: "I went up to him, and I said, pardon me, Mister Doctor, but I heard you saying those things to that poor little lady, and when you left she started crying. He looked at me, and he didn't say a word. He went back to his writing in someone's chart. I felt a rush to my head. I heard my daughter telling me to get on out of that room, but I heard another voice, and it was a higher command, and I went up to that doctor and I told him he was a case himself—of the bad manners; and it's a no good disease to have. He told me to shut up and go away. I told him he could tell me to *git*, but he couldn't tell that to Jesus Christ, our Lord, who was a doctor Himself, and He watches all of us, what we do. Then he told the nurse to fire me. And she said she would call up the office and tell them. I knew I was going. But I remembered Jesus in the temple, and I knew I had to prove myself worthy of Him, so I just did it. I took the tray, with the water in it, and instead of taking it to the patient, like I was supposed to do, I took it to that doctor. I soaked him good! And I prayed for him: I told him his soul meant more than a wet shirt and a wet tie. I told the nurses not to be upset. God will take them, too, if they want to come to Him. And I left before they knew what to say, or what to do. I prayed for them all the way home. The only thing was, I kept thinking that I'd have liked to get my hands on that doctor, and shake him hard. So, I prayed to God that He forgive me my thoughts. There's the devil in me; for sure there is."

For us Ruth Ann was a woman of great strength and conviction whose mental and spiritual life constantly confronted our own. Out of a legacy of extreme poverty, oppression, ignorance, she had fashioned a life of moral concern and reflection. She dared look at the world candidly, boldly, and not least, *sub specie aeternitatis*. A humble, uneducated, sassy, uppity nigger, she was an instrument, we began to feel, of something, if not Someone, larger. Her granddaughter, whom we knew well, felt that the doctors and nurses at the hospital would, in the long run of things, come to agree—though the presumed basis for such a change of opinion (the political, then social acceptance of integration) did not seem to be the point in question. A white "attendant," smitten by Jesus, and bold enough to hurl water on His behalf, would also have been fired. But to risk being presumptuous, "the writer" might indeed have come to appreciate Ruth Ann, who possessed a mixture of extreme seriousness and wry detachment that Dante had in mind when he used the title *Divine Comedy* for his literary and religious effort.

Once Ruth Ann told us that she never wanted to go North; that she was a "southerner through and through"; that she wanted to "meet" her God on her own turf; that she hoped she'd be awake and ready to absorb in its entirety the full significance of that moment, that ultimate event in her, in anyone's life: "When I meet Him, I may discover that I'm headed for Hell, to stay there a long time. He'll come with a sword, you know. The Bible tells us that. He'll have his witnesses, and they'll tell Him the truth. I may just go up in flames. I may just end up in an ocean—on the bottom, staring at some big octopus. One minister said an octopus is the Devil; and he showed us in church what an octopus looks like. I'll be walking on a rainy day, and I see a puddle, and I think of an octopus coming at me, and never letting go. Of course, it would need big arms. Imagine the size of those arms, if they're going to wrap me up (me, with my arms!) and hold me for the rest of time! I had a dream once. The octopus was red, and not black, and he got me, but I stared at the eye, and I kept pushing, and I was too much for him. He let me go! Then I was back at my daddy's working on the cotton with him, but the bossman's plane flew over us, and it was dusting the land with the insect killer stuff, and it came right over us, and it let out a rope, and the rope touched me and it wrapped me up, and the next thing I knew, it was an octopus, a flying octopus, and I woke up. I told my daughter and my granddaughter, and they said that was a terrible dream. But I didn't mind, except for one thing: the flying octopus suddenly changed color; it became purple. That's a scary color."

The dreamer was no Flannery O'Conner, but she lived in the state of Georgia; she grew up in the backcountry of that state; she was deadly serious about not only her particular life, but Life; and she had a storyteller's narrative urgency, dramatic sense, and implicit respect for the possibilities of irony, if not humor. Put differently, the two women were (Ruth Ann has also died) southerners, and neither of them was at all anxious to forsake what that designation meant—a certain kind of experience that shapes the mind's perceiving, reflecting life. Even as Ruth Ann summoned particular words, phrases, images, symbols, memories, day-by-day habits and customs, as she went about her household duties, her preaching life as a lay minister of the gospel, her working life in a hospital (and before that, a factory, and way back, on a plantation as a field hand) the woman she called "the writer" also had within grasp a certain range of ideas and rituals, verbal constructions, and metaphysical notions. The South of "Good Country People," of "The Artificial Nigger," of "Revelation," of *Wise Blood* and *The Violent Bear It Away*, is the concrete South that Ruth Ann and Flannery O'Connor shared, loved, saw changing, knew had to change, stood by as well as laughed at, scorned. And that South is not only a region of a nation, but part of what Ruth Ann kept referring to as "God's Kingdom." She was unrelenting in that regard, unrelenting in her faith that such a kingdom exists—as unrelenting as the driven characters Flannery O'Connor kept sending into the world.

"You keep on talking about 'the South,'" Ruth Ann once told me with obvious impatience and barely controlled exasperation, "but you don't seem to know that the South belongs to God. He's the one we have to look out for in the end: the colored and the white, the rich and the poor, it don't make no difference. My granddaughter is leading our race into the white schools, and I'm mighty proud of her. But I'll tell you, I keep saying to her that here in Atlanta it's just the start. There's other gates to go through, and it won't be your skin, colored or white, that will get you in or keep you out. You asked me a while ago if I'd ever thought of living up North. Yes, I have. But most of the time I've thought of the trip I'll be taking when I die. I'll be going farther away than 'North.' That's the trip you should keep on your mind."

A talkative, imaginative, assertive person, all too intensely preoccupied with God, Christ, the Devil, churches, ministers, the Bible and those whose words appear in it? Oh yes, as she would say it—without reluctance, and certainly, with passion. Flannery O'Connor by no means looked like her; nor, one suspects, did "the writer" have a personality like Ruth Ann's. But they both took for granted quite willingly where they came from, where they were; and they both worried a great deal about where they were going—a migration not at all defined by something called the Mason and Dixon Line. And they shared, one gathers from *Mystery and Manners* and from *The Habit of Being* (Flannery O'Connor's letters, edited by Sally Fitzgerald), a certain defensive pride, a certain truculent insistence upon their right to set ground rules for themselves. The sharecropper's daughter who could tell her granddaughter, an acclaimed heroine of integration, what "really matters," what counts in the long run of "God's judgment," is kin to "the writer" who dared give her northern readers, all caught up in the heady activism of the early 1960s, a story such as "Everything That Rises Must Converge." How well it wears today; how well Ruth Ann's warnings and worries do (and how poorly some of the naïve rhetoric generated by my kind stands up). The displaced, secular, messianic convictions that a black Georgia woman could sense in her bones, a white Georgia woman spotted and raced to capture in a story's tight-knit net.

On one score, however, these two southerners have fared differently. Ruth Ann Jackson attracted a good deal of attention from a rather well-educated, sophisticated Atlanta white audience only once, or at most twice: when school desegregation was being planned, and when she confronted a hospital with her ethical mandate. Such brief notice has to be compared with the scrutiny, the notoriety, the rapt (deservedly, I believe) attention Flannery O'Connor received both in her lifetime, and without letup since her death, in 1964, at the age of thirty-nine. I count in my library ten books, and two major and widely distributed monographs devoted to an understanding of her work. There are dozens and dozens of articles. Doctoral theses continue to accumulate. She is due yet another bibliographical essay, which would have to be substantial—and would quickly be outdated. An authorized biography by her good and wise friend, Sally Fitzgerald, is in the works. How much more critical attention can a couple of dozen stories and two quite slim novels, however brilliantly and originally crafted, manage to sustain—without some recognition from all of us that the time has come for a bit of a pause?

I have been going back to Flannery O'Connor's stories and two novels for a long time; and have also been teaching them for years—since I came back North in the late 1960s. I had not intended to write any extended piece on her work, though I keep referring to her in what I do write, and have to answer to her spirit as I give lectures on her in one course, and in a seminar field questions by students who take to her eagerly, perhaps too much so; or sometimes, refuse altogether what she has to offer. I have also used her nonfiction, the essays collected under the title *Mystery and Manners*—an attempt on her part to locate herself regionally, aesthetically, and not least, theologically. That book has, understandably, not received the attention of its author's fiction, though in it is to be found a quite powerful and distinctive voice—speaking about man and God, the South and twentieth-century America, our culture and our values, with an intelligence, a shrewdness, a hard skepticism and an unyielding religious faith that are, collectively, rare indeed among us these days. My students have found it useful to move back and forth—from O'Connor's fiction to her essays on fiction; from the southern people she has created out of her head, to the South she evokes and tries to comprehend in her nonfiction pieces. And I have followed suit—supposedly the teacher, but often enough responding to a suggestion here, a pointed question there. One of those students, from Rome, Georgia, decided one day to leave on my desk an announcement of the forthcoming publication of Flannery O'Connor's letters, with a recommendation that I write a review. I would thereby live up to a promise I'd been making to myself for some time, that I try to come to terms with her work in a small way, drawing upon my own work in counties such as Baldwin County, Georgia, where she spent most of her life.

An invitation from the faculty of Louisiana State University to deliver the annual Walter Lynwood Fleming Lectures in Southern History became the occasion for an attempt to write down some thoughts about a writer I had admired for a long time, taught, read and reread; a writer to whom, I'd best acknowledge right off, I feel close spiritually—even as I have loved living and working in her native region. Moreover, the publication of *The Habit of Being* has given some real and substantive merit for additional comment on Flannery O'Connor; she was a prolific letter writer, and in that correspondence she did more than offer pleasantries, though she did that, too. She delivered herself of carefully reasoned social comment, philosophical and theological analysis, literary and personal opinion. This is an extensive (some six hundred pages, longer than any of her books) effort at communication by a writer who obviously had a head crammed full of important and luminous thoughts, ideas, beliefs, not to mention plots and subplots; nor would she ever have denied it—strong objections, dislikes, biases. And what she wrote to her friends, or to those who sought her out through the mail, bears directly on what she wrote in her stories, novels, and essays. She was not loath as a correspondent to anticipate a written lecture, or comment in advance or retrospectively about the imaginative constructions she worked on so intensely in the Milledgeville farm, Andalusia. There has always been every reason to take seriously her views on religion, on the South she observed so keenly; also of importance was her continuing struggle to be an actively reasoning person, while at the same time critical of what she regarded in her fellow intellectuals as false, pretentious, stupid. With the publication of her correspondence, there is even more reason to take a look at her along those lines: a somewhat different southern writer; a writer in touch with a region's quite special religious sensibility; and an intellectual who had grave misgivings, which she did not hesitate to express, about her own kind.

No psychological study will ever really "explain" how a novelist pulls together elements of observed reality, the subjective whirl of imaginative life, and the intellect's evaluating, approving, censoring activity—and does so in such a fashion that exquisite control lives side by side with extravagant rumination or demonic indulgence or humorous excess. Freud was wise to surrender before Dostoievski's achievement—yet it was not a defeat others in the psychoanalytic tradition have accepted without bitterness, retaliatory resentment, or dreams of vengeance extracted at some future time. Nor have various members of my profession failed to take on all sorts of writers—as if their emotional troubles (the possession of everyone) will, if correctly appraised, yield up the secret of a particular quarry: the art of fiction, realized and realized again, through a lifetime of effort. Certainly, one can see various psychological themes in a given writer's work—and even connect them to a given life, his or her personal story. And the letters, the recorded statements, the recollected remarks, of that man or woman can tell us more: he or she, again, as struggling with *X* or *Y* or *Z* emotions. But that is as far as it goes; we dance and dance and dance around a magical circle, but we are never going to cross over a certain elusive, invisible boundary line—the fertile energy of a *creating*, not a troubled mind.

Milledgeville, with its state mental hospital, constantly has in its territorial domain thousands of fevered minds, all full of grotesque visions, wild daydreams, and problems galore—men and women at war with mothers, with fathers, with children, with their own consciences or their unconscious excesses of various kinds. To say that

Flannery O'Connor showed signs of this or that "problem," as revealed by her writing, fiction or nonfiction, is to say that she was yet another human being on this earth. Any southern town—or northern city—is full of people contending with tensions, rivalries, worries, fears, hates, passions. All that emotional energy doesn't fuel, in those countless millions, even a sentence or two such as Flannery O'Connor could write when she was—not "acting out" or "expressing" or "sublimating" a "problem," not making some psychological connection between the themes in her mental life and the themes in the fiction she produced, but moving from the immanence we all know to a quite particular form of transcendence, to draw on a mode of analysis older than the twentieth-century psychodynamic variety. So much for a "psychological approach" to this writer, or any other one.

Flannery O'Connor was not only especially aware of herself as a southerner; she had, rare for someone from Georgia writing in the 1950s and 1960s, a distinctly historical view of what obtained about her—a view several of her stories maintain, and her letters, her essays, amplify considerably. To be sure, her Thomism, and at the end of her life, the writing of Pierre Teilhard de Chardin, were encouraging in that regard. But so was her literary sensibility; she was, after all, on Hawthorne's side, rather than Emerson's and Thoreau's—to draw upon a Yankee polarity. That is to say, she was skeptical about the possibilities of human nature, distrustful of any age's or social order's showy self-confidence, and inclined to satirize the present, while doubting the promises of those who look to a new kind of future. Put differently, she was a conservative in a sense of that word not available to many of us today; she distrusted many of her own generation's enthusiasms. She favored detachment in a world whose assumptions she often challenged strenuously. The secular messianic mentality was not hers; she mocked it—a critically important element in her writing. But she wasn't sitting on a plantation with a gun, daring some federal marshals to come get her. As she repeatedly pointed out, her fiction was peopled by the hard-pressed poor, to whom she felt Christ's kind of kinship—even as she remembered that one of His loyal disciples, of all people, would deny Him three times; and upon that follower, the Church of Rome would be built. Such built-in historical ironies never receded from her mind's range of vision.

Her theological interests have, of course, received important and continuing recognition. But there is room for further inquiry into the kind of Catholicism she called upon *as a writer*. Her debt to St. Thomas, and in our century, Jacques Maritain, and again, Teilhard de Chardin, has been examined carefully. However, even the fine, theologically sensitive scrutiny given her in *The Eternal Crossroads* fails to mention another side of her Catholicism—perhaps because she was less explicit in her public acknowledgment of it. In her correspondence she tells of the influence Georges Bernanos had on her; she read him carefully, and more than once went over *The Diary of a Country Priest* with special care. Moreover, the Catholic convert Edith Stein, and the Catholic spirit (or should I say the Catholic nonconvert, the Catholic heretic?) Simone Weil obviously entranced her. These two exceptional Jewesses deserve a place in the critical O'Connor literature, and so does the idiosyncratic literary pilgrimage of Bernanos. *The Habit of Being* is indispensable in that regard, as it is in giving us an idea of the intellectual breadth and depth of this southern writer—and of her peculiar struggles with that very achievement. "It ain't no fun being a smart nigger around here," Ruth Ann Jackson once told us in a rare moment of despair—and arguably, pride. Her predicament in several respects was not completely unlike that of the woman she knew as "the writer"; and what they both have to tell us about the South and its history is, needless to say, one of our chief concerns in the pages to follow.

I come to Flannery O'Connor's work with affection and respect. I mean these comments as an homage. I have spent years in the homes of people who are, in certain respects, her chosen ones—the South's impoverished, hard-praying, stubbornly enduring rural folk, of both races. She knew them all right—not as a distant population, to be exposed or exploited or dismissed with condescension or stern disapproval (yet another "them"), but as neighbors, as fellow travelers on a road whose destination she would never for long allow her mind to forget. She learned from the people she watched so intently, heard so well; and she wanted her readers to do likewise—learn, while having fun with good stories. When some of those readers dismissed a certain rural landscape, powerfully evoked, as pitiable, eccentric, grotesque, she was quick to respond—not "defensively" or with chauvinism, but as a student who knew whereof she spoke; and she had done some comparative ("cross-cultural") fieldwork: a residence up North. Modesty and a scrupulous honesty denied her the easy and glib access other visitors have found to various, distant worlds. She was not one to wander, assimilate anything and everything, make all worlds her world. Even on her native soil she took exceeding care to connect only with those she found familiar. I hope to show what social scene in the South she did call upon, and do so in a way that echoes her terribly important, unforgettable comment: "I have found that anything that comes out of the South is going to be called grotesque by the northern reader, unless it is grotesque, in which case it is going to be called realistic." She aimed to confront others through *their* distortions, as well as to make a few of her own. Who is distorting whom, and why—those were the questions she asked, and ones that ought be considered by those of us who read her or think about the persisting question of regionalism within this country.

I dedicate this book to two long-time friends. Years ago Richard Poirier appreciated the stormy, eruptive power of Flannery O'Connor. He watched her emerge as an artist. He read her closely. He chose her stories for prizes. I have been lucky, privileged to know him for two decades. He has taught me a lot. He is a good, good friend. I salute him warmly. I do so to David Riesman, as well—whom I've known since I returned from the South, and whose letters have straightened out my mind again and again. Miss O'Connor had no great love for social science, and she knew precisely why—the prideful excess of generalization to be found in some of the sociological and psychological journals. She fought hard for the concrete, the particular—to the point that, thereby, her point of view as a writer of fiction was shaped. I believe her spirit quite congenial to David Riesman's, because his career as a sociologist, essayist, observer of his fellow citizens, has been characterized by a remarkably brilliant and faithful dedication to the specifics of American life. He is one constantly to zigzag, commonly to turn coins over, reverse directions, show exceptions to this or that (all too ready, all too accepted) rule of thumb. He has spotted, over and over, the parochialism of those who feel themselves in rightful possession of the power to declare who is and is not parochial. I believe this is the right place to acknowledge the informal and extended instruction he has offered me for well over a decade. I audited his course. He graciously permitted me to attend the weekly meetings he held with the teaching associates of that course. His letters, as his many correspondents know, are a treasure to have—and I hope and pray some future Sally Fitzgerald will try to do justice to the "habit" of *his* "being."

Speaking of Sally Fitzgerald, I must with gratitude and great pleasure testify to the enormous assistance she lent me as I contemplated, then undertook this writing project. Our conversations were extremely helpful, suggestive. So were those with Robert Fitzgerald. So was the time I spent with Regina Cline O'Connor in Milledgeville, at her home in town, and at Andalusia. So were the hours spent with Gerald Becham, who takes care of Miss O'Connor's books and papers at Georgia College. With the Fitzgeralds, I am lucky indeed that my friendships connect to those of Flannery O'Connor's—and similarly with Louise Abbot, who knew and corresponded with the woman Ruth Ann introduced my wife to as "the writer, from down there in Baldwin County." I have been very much helped by Louise Abbot's "Remembering Flannery," and by her letters to me—and also by her cousin, Alvin Neely, an old, old friend of my wife's and mine, going back to our Vinings days. Alvin was also specifically helpful when I was preparing myself for this work. He lives in Savannah, knows "kin of Flannery's"—took me around, so to speak. (He is no stranger to Andalusia, either.) Years ago, I spoke with Walker Percy about Flannery O'Connor and was helped by so doing. I mentioned her in the introduction to the study I made of Dr. Percy (*Walker Percy: An American Search*) this way: "I connect Dr. Percy, maybe out of my own peculiar inclinations, with another southerner, Flannery O'Connor, and with two French writers, Simone Weil and Georges Bernanos—four Catholic travelers of serious purpose indeed." I went on to express a hope that I would be able, in my limited way, to come to terms with them; as Gabriel Marcel said it, to "respond" to them as an act of faith—a faith one shares with them, a faith one wants to express through an amen of sorts to their strong articulations.

And finally the faculty of Louisiana State University, and the members of its Press: I thank them for the kindness of their invitation, for their considerable, memorable hospitality, for giving me, again, an occasion in which to bring these thoughts together. I was no stranger to Baton Rouge when I came there in the Spring of 1979. I remembered, then, other moments—with SNCC workers, whom I visited in the East Baton Rouge Parish prison (Dion Diamond, for one) and on behalf of whom I had to testify time and again. That was a different Baton Rouge, a different Louisiana—in 1961, 1962, 1963—and we all have real reason to be right pleased in 1979, though, keeping the spirit of Flannery O'Connor in mind, not wide-eyed with innocent (and prideful) hope.

ONE

THE SOCIAL SCENE

FLANNERY O'CONNOR'S REMARK quoted in the Introduction, about the perception of the grotesque, was an accusation. She believed that the South is inevitably distorted in the minds of the northern reader. Perhaps she was herself making a distortion of sorts, if not a rather too inclusive generalization. Which northern readers? Don't they vary? Weren't some of them able to see what she was about? Still, her complaint was not grounded exclusively in animus or grudge. She had plenty of reason, by the autumn of 1960, when she made the assertion, to believe herself thoroughly misunderstood—as one who gratuitously served up the bizarre from a land full of such. So believing, she was yet another southerner, all too aware of the inclination others have to make a mockery of a region's life. Nor have the aggrieved southerners only been writers, teachers, the thoroughly educated. It is important, I believe, to connect Flannery O'Connor's view of her native region, and her view of the Yankees' view of that region, with the perceptions of others—so-called ordinary people who come from states such as Georgia, Alabama, Mississippi, Louisiana.

"A facility for fiction," she told one of her correspondents, "depends on the ability to mimic the social scene." She had the knack all right. She knew how her people felt, acted—including those whose northern stay has become too influential. Mary Grace, the eighteen- or nineteen-year-old Wellesley College student in "Revelation" is enraged by the conversation she hears, as she reads her textbook *Human Development*: smalltown, ignorant, trashy talk—pointless babble. When Asbury of "The Enduring Chill" comes back from New York City, in his midtwenties and sick, he is hardly appreciative of Timberboro, his hometown; nor does his mother fail to appreciate that fact. Her son has told her that "they have better doctors in New York." She replies that a hometown doctor "would take a personal interest" in him. Regional distinctions apply to medical practice, the argument goes: knowledge as against familiarity. But that polarization is itself a distortion—so many southerners, regardless of class or race, would want to argue. They would also point out that when such a slanderous notion is left unchallenged, the designation *grotesque* is the next step—a label not only slapped on Timberboro's (the rural South's) professional life, but just about anything that goes on "down there."

The northern reader is, of course, in for a treacherous time with Miss O'Connor's stories. It is too easy for a Yankee to identify rather quickly with the expatriate, who has to suffer a return to the smothering narrowness of village life—to confront, as the story moves on, his or her moral and philosophical limits. Naturally, such a turn of events takes place in the O'Connor canon within the "social scene" she refers to: the daily events of "backwoods" life. By the time we have visited a doctor's office here ("Revelation"), a mother and son there ("The Enduring Chill," "Everything That Rises Must Converge"), we have begun to suspect that those southern towns and cities deserve the reputation they have among certain Yankees, or expatriates come home. Whose vision is distorted, provincial? That of New Yorkers, of New Englanders, who have their own kinds of ugliness, blindness, meanness of spirit—while regarding the South's Timberboros as repositories of ignorance and hate? That of southerners, who show plenty of foibles and worse, but are constantly misinterpreted or subject to galling condescension?

I suspect that if Flannery O'Connor had made a woman such as Mrs. Fox, Asbury's mother, a black, the northern reader would be less inclined to find her a gratuitously interfering, possessive woman—a representation of the old, stiff-necked, smalltown South. Many of us would shift the lenses in our microscope, characterize her as proud, defiantly herself, unyielding in the face of intrusions of various kinds, including those supplied by her own son. But I am suggesting another story. Miss O'Connor never made blacks the central figures in her stories. Nor, really, did she get into the heads of Yankees, either. She knew which "social scene" was hers: not the upper-class South; not really, with a few exceptions, its professional and business cadres; but overwhelmingly, its "poor white" rural and smalltown folk, or its ordinary working-class men and women, some of whom, admittedly, do have their higher aspirations. When there is an "aristocrat" (as in "Everything That Rises Must Converge"), it is one who is virtually at the end of the line—shabby gentility.

In any event, I'd like to introduce here an echoing voice of sorts, one which, I believe, will underscore what Miss O'Connor had in mind when she rendered her charge against Yankee readers, and maybe, a few from her native region. And had in mind as she worked into her stories the above-described tensions between the Yankees (knowing) world and the South's pietistic, gossipy, superstitious people who ramble on and on, or make nuisances of themselves, or mouth ignorant or banal comments, to the annoyance of the (Yankee influenced) cognoscenti. Here is a Georgia black woman talking about friendly, decent, honorable, idealistic civil rights workers, come to help her and members of her family and their neighbors to vote. The year is 1962, the place the southern part of Georgia: Dougherty County—Albany, to be exact. The speaker is a follower of Dr. Martin Luther King's, so no "white man's nigger." Her son has, unlike Asbury, never gone North; but she worries that he will—worries for reasons not unlike those Mrs. Fox might have had before her son left. And she worries, as Mrs. Fox did, about the contrast between a rural southern town and a northern big city: "I hear all those nice civil rights people from up there talk about us folks down here, and I get a sore head. No matter if they're white or if they're black, they talk down to us. They make us out to be slow moving and with not the brains we should have. I wish we could get some help from people who don't mistake the way we are. They come here, and they want to lift us up to their level. Well, we need some lifting, I can't deny it. But so do a lot of people, including some who live in New York City, New York, and Chicago, Illinois. I pray for them up North, just like I pray for us, down here. I'll tell you why: we're all in danger of going to Hell."

The theological side of her remarks deserve attention; we will come back to them. For now, it is her sectional pride that deserves respect. A southern country woman, she knew her people's needs: all possible assistance, direct and immediate. Moreover, the help could only come from outside the region—hard to take, if one feels a streak of associated condescension arriving with what one knows is necessary. Her minister had told her this, and she could not forget it: "We can scream and holler down here; we can go to jail and go to jail. We've been screaming and hollering for years; we've been going to jail for years; I've seen our people strung up on trees, and lying dead in ditches. And it hasn't made any difference, none at all. But if they start hearing up North; if they pay attention to us; if they come down here and start joining us—then that's *something*, oh is it! Every colored person here, and every white person will know the difference. When the North decides you're on the map, you're on the map; and when the North has someone else to worry about—well, you might just as well stop your worrying about yourself, and go about your business, the best you can."

North of her by a few dozen miles a writer would have smiled at that expression, "go about your business." She was always referring to it as "bidniss," the way some white and black country people do. But in my experience, the pronunciation varies: those better educated by virtue not of schooling, but a ministerial connection (a relative, a friend, a neighbor, or an attentive parishioner), tend to favor a clear-cut approach to the word. That same writer would surely have nodded in agreement with the black woman's viewpoint. What goes for those in the civil rights movement, goes for others as well. Writers as well as political activists crave audiences, crave approval, crave the acceptance of knowing, influential men and women. When the North gives its nod to a southern writer, a lot begins to take place: a reputation is established; the person is on his or her way. And without such notice, life can be hard, frustrating, quite literally unrewarding. It is against such a "reality" that Flannery O'Connor and the black tenant farmer quoted above found themselves, at times, constrained to speak. And with them, generations of southerners, no matter their background, occupation, racial stock.

The issue is, I suppose, power; and Miss O'Connor was politely but firmly pointing out that someone, someplace, owns the word *grotesque*, a deviant child of that parent entity, *normal*. Surely neither she, nor other Georgia writers, nor the black rural field hands of the state, have ever had much say in the matter of what in this nation is and is not considered "appropriate," "seemly," "desirable," let alone "grotesque." The standards come from elsewhere. A good appraisal was once included in some sociological ruminations of the black minister who taught the above south Georgia black woman "the facts of life," as she called them, and who also knew precisely why he wanted Dr. Martin Luther King's help in the early 1960s: "If you want to know how change begins to work, you have to go North. The change starts in New York, and it starts in Washington, and then it reaches Atlanta, and if it's going strong, it moves down through our state—and here we are, way down; but it gets here, if there's the push from up there."

He might be considered a scholar in the study of the diffusion of political power; certainly he knew how to get his message across to those predominantly illiterate, frightened and toughly skeptical (why not?) field hands—who, maybe, knew what he meant all along, though without exact understanding of the urban designations he chose to offer. It can be uncanny, out there in that "anthropological field," so-called—hearing people without education referring to "the mysterious ways of God," and referring to His "principalities and powers." There is, naturally, a secular application to such phrases; and for a Milledgeville, Georgia, writer, or an Albany, Georgia, preacher, or a Dougherty County, Georgia, field hand, the compass still offers the best help for those who want to fit the Bible's language into today's life: North as against South.

At another point in *Mystery and Manners*, Miss O'Connor allows herself this historical and sociological generalization: "The South is traditionally hostile to outsiders, except on her own terms. She is traditionally against intruders, foreigners from Chicago or New Jersey, all those who come from afar with moral energy that increases in direct proportion to the distance from home." One can feel a certain bitterness in those two sentences, delivered in Washington, D.C. during the fateful year 1963, just before the writer's last struggle with lupus—and when the civil rights movement was marching all over, including the nation's capital, where thousands and thousands of black and white citizens stood on the Congressional Mall and before Lincoln's statue with a demand for "freedom, freedom now." As if she is worried lest she be misinterpreted, we are given this qualification and amplification: "It is difficult to separate the virtues of this quality from the narrowness which accompanies it for the outside world. It is more difficult still to reconcile the South's instinct to preserve her identity with her equal instinct to fall eager victim to every poisonous breath from Hollywood or Madison Avenue."

How much has she given ground? Is the narrowness, in fact, present —or is it, again, something in the Yankee beholder's eye? The preposition *for* is used ambiguously. Not that Miss O'Connor's stories don't show "narrowness"—what her readers, at least, would see as such. The two novels abound in fierce dogmatism, in impatient and simple-minded pursuits of various kinds. Mrs. Freeman and Mrs. Hopewell, in "Good Country People," are hardly the broad-minded, worldly wise ones of this world. Julian's mother, in "Everything That Rises Must Converge," qualifies as "narrow"; and, of course, poor Parker in "Parker's Back" has a wife who must be one of the least forgiving religious zealots in all literature. But who are the readers who will be making those judgments? Miss O'Connor may have been asking that question implicitly. She knew that her readers, even those who applauded her most eagerly, were predominantly well-educated, agnostic Yankees, who found her a brilliant storyteller, and were more than willing—in their broad-mindedness, their *lack* of narrowness—to put up with the likes of Hazel Motes (*Wise Blood*) or old Mason Tarwater, and his nephew Francis Marion Tarwater (*The Violent Bear It Away*).

These driven or frustrated religious prophets are, no doubt about it, part of the region's traditional life. But in fact such prophets have no less "moral energy" than Yankee political activists—who are not wont to hear themselves described as "narrow" upon arriving in the South, or certainly, upon returning home. I am being now a bit evasive myself: *hear themselves*. I'm afraid a few things have been said—heard or unheard. To draw from our black woman from south Georgia—now speaking in 1966, two years after Flannery O'Connor lost her chance to reconsider her somewhat "defensive" posture about the South and its visitors from afar: "They were a big help. We couldn't have done it without the outsiders who came here. I don't know if I'd ever pick myself up and go clear across the country, to fight some sheriff and his men. We had three people from California here; we had three from Massachusetts. They paid their way to come, and they supported themselves while they stayed. If that isn't being a friend, what is!

"Of course, they weren't angels. No one is, not a man or woman alive. They had the devil in them, like all of us do. Talk, they talked and talked. They told us this, and they told us that. They made us feel nothing was working right. My stove was in bad shape, they said. I wasn't serving my kids the right food. We needed to do better with our teeth. And they were always worrying about worms and bugs and smells and—even the water got them going against us. The schools, too: bad books and bad teachers and a bad building. It was all bad—our roads, and our food store and the poor undertaker, who was cheating us out of everything, they told us, and the insurance man. They was right a lot of the time; I can't deny it. But they stirred up a storm. We were fighting the white man, but meanwhile, we began fighting each other, the colored who were 'exploiting,' and the colored who were 'the victim.' My husband said it was getting so that he couldn't think of any of our neighbors, without calling them a name to himself. We lost our favorite schoolteacher. She said she was going up to Atlanta, and she'd study at Atlanta University. She was tired of being called an Uncle Tom. She wasn't a bad soul. Maybe she should have fought with the court people, over the books we got, all used and torn and nowhere the equal of what the white people's children got for themselves. But she'd have been fired, pronto—one disagreeing whisper from her, and that would have been the end. Sure, it's changing now. Like I say, we needed the outside people to help us do it; they could tell anyone off, and they didn't have to be afraid of no one firing them, and riding them out of the country. The sheriff knew better than to try—not with all those television people around, and their cameras.

"I'll tell you something: I don't want to sound like I can't remember a good turn. I say it now, and I'll repeat it tomorrow, and I'll always say it: they helped us. But I'm glad they're gone. Why? I'll put my answer before you, on this table of ours: they had too high an opinion of themselves, some of those outsiders we had here, staying with us. They tried to boost us up; I know. But after a while, we were in as bad shape with them as with the sheriff and his people. My husband said to me one morning: we're exchanging one set of white folks for another. And the colored students who came here, some of them were more white than the white. I should have my tongue cut out for talking like that. I know I should. Where would we be without them? But, like our minister tells us, the Bible says there's a time for the sun to come up, and there's a time for the sun to go down, and there was a time for those people to come here and give us all they had, and scold us, too, and there was a time for them to say goodbye, and leave us be here. And we can scold ourselves. And, maybe, they'll learn to scold themselves—but don't count on it! That's not in their natures to do. They're much better at finding folks like us to scold! There I go again with my bad-mouthing talk! I'll have a sorry time when I pass. The Lord will have the record of my words, and *He'll* do some scolding, too!"

One listens and listens, and later on, cuts through extended conversations, changing a few grammatical constructions on the way—all for what? A notion, one hopes, of how a much-abused people took to a redemptive moment in their history. Those are not the words of a slyly covert segregationist, nor the remarks of a member of the southern, rural brand of E. Franklin Frazier's "black bourgeoisie." The views are laced with self-criticism; are not offered smugly or without a distinct and low bow to the complexities, the ambiguities, the ironies of recent southern history. A black tenant farmer and his wife saw idealism at work, but also a touch of hauteur, a mite stain of the "narrowness" Miss O'Connor mentioned. A narrowness, it was, that had to do with noblesse oblige: we are saviors of sorts, so pay us heed. Too harsh a judgment? An easy appraisal to make over a decade later, when a fierce struggle is over? The nit-picking of an academic mind greedy for its own, self-important position to stake out—that of the even-handed memorialist, who claims a right to forget the urgencies of the past, and concentrate on the small, abrasive moments, inevitable in a social revolution?

Maybe so, in my case; but I cannot forget those moments, because they were rather more numerous than I wished at the time. And I'd better bring in a white voice, too—in view of the subject matter at hand. A man whose large Georgia family might be described as "good country people" was a neighbor of ours in Cobb County, and with a little whiskey in him, gave us his thoughts at great length: "They come down here, and they tell us we're no good, and they're going to change everything around. Half of them have never seen a colored person in their lives. The other half has one colored friend and two distant acquaintances. What do they know about Georgia? Who's asked them to take a test about their own backyards? Could they pass the test? I was up North during the war; I know what Chicago is like. They can have Chicago, and New York and all those places. The day will come, let me say it right now [1962] when we'll have solved this whole thing, right down here, person to person and neighbor to neighbor, and they won't even know where to begin up there.

"We have good colored folks down here; the bad ones have gone and left us, and good riddance to them. They don't want this integration thing; it's an *idea*, that's what it is, in the heads of those people up there—so full of themselves, they can't see anyone else. You think the niggers here really trust these agitators? You think the colored people don't know who's here to stay, and who's just passing through—looking for a *cause*. That's what the real problem is: you have a bunch of college kids, a lot of them pretty rich, and living in homes one million miles from the nearest colored family. And these kids have a lot of time on their hands, and too much energy, and they love to find people to look down on, and people who will look up to them as it each and every one of them was Jesus Christ Himself. So, they say to each other: let's go South, and have us a damn good time down there, with all those dumb crackers.

"There will come a day when the shoe will be on the other foot, and all the trouble we have down here won't look so bad, when you see what's going on up there. And when that day comes, I'll promise you something: no one from Georgia is going to go up there, pointing his finger at people, and telling them they're no good, and they're ignorant, and they have to change by federal law, or else. It's not our way, down here, to go poking into the business of others, so we can have our fun. If those people would take themselves to church, other than to organize integration rallies, while they're down here staying among us, they might learn something—about pride, the worst sin of all. But they'd laugh if I went and told them that—because I didn't go to college. And if I had gone, it would have been to Georgia Tech, not Harvard. I wish I could have gone to Georgia Tech; but I didn't have the dough when I was young. My daddy died when I was ten. I've been working ever since. So, what do I know? They wouldn't listen to me; I'm just a dumb Georgia redneck to them, a six-pack boy! And some nigger they adopt, what's he but a teacher's pet of theirs, someone to pin on their 'Look What I Did' wall!"

Harsh, mean talk; the words of someone who felt himself accused, and was ready to strike out, rather than acknowledge that maybe there was a case to be made by those from the South *and* those from the North then involved in confronting people like him everywhere, it seemed. Still, he has turned out not to be the worst prophet in the world. His children have attended integrated schools, and his neighbors up the road have always been black people. The intimacy of the races is something he has always taken for granted, and still does: the South's rural lowlife, a cynical social observer with a categorical mind might say—a kind of living still very much in evidence throughout many counties of Georgia and its sister states of the Southeast. And if there is plenty of disparity, yet, between the region's white and black people, urban or rural, who up North is in a position now to take his or her "moral energy" *South*? For the first time in its history the South has, for only a decade or so, found itself no longer a fit object for the "moral energy" of those "outsiders" who for generations have been coming to states such as Georgia or Louisiana.

The point is not that Flannery O'Connor saw correctly, in the very midst of her region's travail, what was coming around the corner. What matters is the edge she worked against at the time, as worked into her fiction and nonfiction alike—a sense that, apart from the matter of equity, which is what the blacks were concentrating on, there was something else at work, so far as certain white people were concerned: displaced "energy," and no small amount of hypocrisy. Put differently, men and women were looking elsewhere with ease, with considerable gratification, with no small amount of applause, and with objective assurance that they were "doing right"—while the horrors of their own cities and states went unregarded or unmentioned. That discrepancy, regional in nature, caught her attention enough to have a bearing on the fiction she produced—she, who remained at home, kept among the people she knew best, and obviously, loved attending: the white yeomen, the small-town white folk of Georgia, some of whom live in the southern part of the state, with blacks an everyday part of life, and some of whom live in communities clearly meant to be in the mountain part of east Tennessee or north Georgia, where blacks are relatively rare.

The critical literature devoted to Flannery O'Connor's fiction has largely taken for granted the "social scene" she evokes in favor of a needed (and often suggestive) explication of the religious symbols she has employed, the philosophical themes she has tried to develop. If she's used "cracker" people, used their talk and their habits and way of seeing things; if she's thrown in a few observing or quietly put-upon blacks; if she's kept the rural landscape fairly near at hand, in story after story—then that is an instrumental part of a writer's effort, directed at giving us a message, or at the least, discomforting us enough to drive home a few reminders about *our* condition, as opposed to that of the characters (in several senses of the word) we so easily tend to laugh at with pity, feel at a remove from. I shall myself, later on, try to comment on some of the religious issues she struggled with; but I believe the southern world she created has its own integrity—as part of a writer's thematic preoccupation and intent. What is happening in this Southland, she asked—which has become a quite "eager victim" to all the secular blandishments twentieth-century America offers *everyone*? (In my experience, even the most remote Eskimo villages of the Arctic seacoast or the tundra are similarly vulnerable.) Moreover, she asked as a novelist, given that kind of social vulnerability and cultural complicity, what is apt to happen, time and again, to individuals when the poison gets inhaled?

It is easy for some to misconstrue such a purpose. In her correspondence she takes note of the extremely disapproving reviews she received over the years. Was she a gratuitously cruel, callous, and politically reactionary writer, able with apparent aplomb to wipe out a vacationing family at the hands of a "misfit"; able to let a supposedly intelligent, well-bred woman stand helplessly silent while a tractor kills one of her employees; able to mock the motives of a white man willing to join the cause of (bus) integration—and in a story that appeared at a time when precious few whites were willing to break with their segregationist past, no matter their motives; able to turn a thoughtful, well-read woman into a snotty fool, who is conned down to the stump of her leg, while her mother and her mother's friend and neighbor exchange stupid or evil banalities, world without end, it seems—but without harm or ridicule to themselves? What are we to make of that South, in its concrete form—never mind the symbolic implications of these various incidents, confrontations, arrangements of fate?

"The Displaced Person," for instance—one of her best-known stories, and the only one, I believe, successfully adapted to film—is indeed a religious drama, by obvious design. Still, even though not dealing with the South in the explicit, historical manner of, say, "A View of the Woods," or "A Late Encounter with the Enemy," Miss O'Connor manages to portray with great power the southern scene. Perhaps she is more effective in "The Displaced Person" than in those stories, precisely because in it she has her mind on other issues than her native South, hence is less given to the driving parody she sustains elsewhere. Still, she has not forsaken either the South or its comic (and at the same time tragic) possibilities in "The Displaced Person." The first sentence offers us the peacock, that historical symbol of Christian transcendence; but we also meet Mrs. Shortley, and the two of them appear to be "a complete procession." We are to learn about an important element in the South, its poor white folk—as it is threatened (a brilliant stroke) not by civil rights demonstrators but a refugee from Europe's midcentury madness: a survivor of Hitler and Stalin named Guizac. Mrs. Shortley, concretely rendered by a writer who wonderfully shunned abstract talk in her stories, is everything the white South appeared to be during the 1950s, on the eve of the racial struggle: "Her arms were folded and as she mounted the prominence, she might have been the giant wife of the countryside, come out at some sign of danger to see what the trouble was. She stood on two tremendous legs, with the grand self-confidence of a mountain, and rose, up narrowing bulges of granite, to two icy blue points of light that pierced forward, surveying everything. She ignored the white afternoon sun which was creeping behind a ragged wall of cloud as if it pretended to be an intruder and cast her gaze down the red clay road that turned off from the highway."

It is, at once, a familiar southern scene, and yet grimly representative: the solid presence of a people *there*—for a long, long time settled on that Georgia land. Yet, a people strangely on guard, ironically open to attack, even defenseless, no matter its sense of its own worth, and its moments of conviction that what was will always be. Hence, a people watchful, wary, anxious to know who is coming, and from what direction, and with what plan in mind. Always ready to mirror our human predicaments through a quick aside devoted to the natural world, the author chooses to enact in a few words what will soon be happening to Mrs. Shortley and a lot of others in the South—a stealthy *nouveau arriviste* will emerge from hiding, heat things up dramatically, show a power (in a flash) to take a central position in everyone's scheme of things. The deceptions permitted by the clouds will no longer work.

I'm no doubt reading things rather closely; but let me follow the author a little further on. The peacock follows Mrs. Shortley—whose family *shortly* will be going through a strong challenge to their situation as tenants on someone's farm. The peacock seems to have its attention "fixed in the distance on something no one else could see." Meanwhile, in a less detached or religious plane of ocular activity, Mrs. Shortley spies a black car coming on the property. So do "the two Negroes," field hands both, with those suggestive names: Astor and Sulk. We are told that they had taken to hiding behind a tree, but they were not by any means fooling Mrs. Shortley. She knew that something potentially disruptive might be coming down the road, and she knew that the blacks knew. Then the boss appears, Mrs. McIntyre, who is smiling and ready to be gracious, but we are told, is a touch "nervous" as well. And she is doing what the *other* "hired help" immediately recognize as something extraordinary—something they can't help comparing to what they might expect, were they arriving as prospective farmhands: "Here was the owner of the place out to welcome them." She was all dressed up, too. Moreover, the Guizacs were announced, so to speak, by a priest. Nor was he leaving anything to guesswork. Mrs. Shortley saw his collar and his black suit and realized that here was a priest who had no interest in blurring the distinction between himself and everyone else. The authority of God—of some people's God, at least—is connected to this arrival. And to make matters more confusing and exceptional, the displaced person doesn't simply take and lightly acknowledge Mrs. McIntyre's proffered hand, he bows and kisses it. Mrs. Shortley knows what would happen if her husband tried anything like that.

Now the wife of the boss-woman's dairyman begins to remember her current events—Europe, the war, concentration camps. In a thrust at the comic absurdity that unspeakable tragedy can become in the minds of many of us, no matter where we live and how much we think we know, the author has Mrs. Shortley remember something she'd once seen. It isn't the easily dismissed "ignorance" or "provinciality" of Mrs. Shortley that is at work. The "poisonous breath" of both Hollywood and Madison Avenue (or is it, to be specific, Avenue of the Americas?) gets documented disarmingly and without the slightest recourse to rhetoric or abstract commentary: "Mrs. Shortley recalled a newsreel she had seen once of a small room piled high with bodies of dead naked people all in a heap, their arms and legs tangled together, a head thrust in here, a head there, a foot, a knee, a part that should have been covered up sticking out, a hand raised clutching nothing. Before you could realize that it was real and take it into your head, the picture changed and a hollow-sounding voice was saying, 'Time marches on!'"

So it does—a banality come home to the rural South in the concrete form of a Polish "D.P." The result is a person's alarmed curiosity turned marvelously into a rising and portentous social force: "Her stomach trembled as if there had been a slight quake in the heart of the mountain and automatically she moved down from her elevation and went forward to be introduced to them, as if she meant to find out at once what they were capable of." We have been told, just before, that Mrs. Shortley had in her mind connected the new arrival with the "murderous ways" the newsreel had briefly shown. What might happen, she wonders, now that such death-tainted individuals are part of American life? Soon enough she is being introduced to Mr. Guizac, and her husband is being summoned. "Chancey's at the barn," she points out; and then she adds this: "He don't have time to rest himself in the bushes like them niggers over there."

We are suddenly, twelve paragraphs into a rather long short story, jolted by that remark. The author has been carefully preparing us for it—an introduction that sets the stage for a brief, grim announcement of the facts of a region's life. The buildup has been historical: Europe's turmoil, years and years of it, and the subsequent migratory response of hundreds of thousands of people, have affected others all over the world, not the least of whom are the Shortleys and their black co-workers. As a scriptwriter for some newsreel might put it: "The South is changing!" And when a place begins to change, a people begins to contemplate what must be done to hold on, to survive. In a brisk, factual comment about where her husband is, and a pointed comparison between him and two co-workers, Mrs. Shortley compresses an entire history of what others, in language evasive and weak, refer to as "race relations." That her husband's name, at just this moment, is revealed to us as Chancey, may be considered a gentle authorial boost for the reader—who is, step by step, being taken up a ladder, from which a rather broad arc of southern landscape can be gained. Life's contingencies do indeed press upon the South's agricultural laborers, especially those who are tenant farmers, or hired hands—historically the overwhelming majority of the region's black and white people. Miss O'Connor knows that when the going gets tough for such people, only a relative handful of even those who regard themselves as tough can, in fact, get going. Instead, they find themselves in jeopardy, threatened by an apparently inscrutable world, which seems, on the whole, anything but kindly in nature.

What is one to think—of oneself, as well as the world, the specific social order of which one is a part? What is one to do? Acquiesce? Pray long and faithfully? Strike out or back in some fashion? And what would one's supposed "betters" do, were they in such an unpromising, if not near disastrous situation? The author of "The Displaced Person" obviously is searching the skies as well as the particular farm Mrs. McIntyre happens to own (for a pitiable speck of time in eternity's scheme of things). But religion is part of the everyday life of sinful human beings; it is a "social scene" that looms over what personal faith we try to muster, not to mention what evil tempts us, tries to win us over. Mrs. Shortley is to be our guide through that "scene." The imagery that has connected her several times to a mountain can be used in different ways, depending upon the reader's taste. One person's notion of massive, stubborn *thereness* can become another person's obscene fat. And when the mountain speaks, many a reader will hear a pig making the disgusting racist noises that have made "Tobacco Road" no mere title of a novel. Moreover, the author cleverly conspires with her readers' prejudices. Mrs. Shortley is given us as follows: "Her look first grazed the tops of the displaced people's heads and then revolved downwards slowly, the way a buzzard glides and drops in the air until it alights on the carcass."

The Gadarene swine of the Bible, we must remember, contained the spirits of devils. The author switches her imagery to introduce us, quite pointedly, to the desperate, driven greed that is part of this natural world—buzzards that fly, and our own kind. The "niggers" are replaced by the two children of the displaced family. The girl and the boy are compared with the Shortleys' two daughters and son. Under duress from the outside, we turn sour inside. We also turn apprehensive—and in no time, begin turning on ourselves. How do we look? How do we measure up? Is there, God forbid, some objective basis, hence justification, for what seems to be happening? That is to say, has the apparently arbitrary, capricious hand of fate really been a response of the world's to one or another evident flaw? Such questions are the stuff of every scared person's daydreams and nightmares. However, when an entire region has had good reason historically to feel precarious about its prospects, not to mention judged sternly by others, a rather more public kind of response takes place.

Miss O'Connor has worked elements of that response into the chain of mental associations her character Mrs. Shortley finds within herself. The threat of an outsider prompts a reminder that the blacks are also outsiders within the motherland, or fatherland—it comes down to the same thing, an extended family of sorts gravely threatened. Then rise the murderous impulses, the hunt for the flesh of a convenient scapegoat. And next, as the buzzard glides and glides within a pinched and prickly soul, the eyes can't help turning their attention to the body they belong to, to nearby blood—"flesh of my flesh." We are told that one of the Shortley daughters, true to that literal sense of her last name, "has never got her growth." The other one had "a cast in her eye." So it has gone, the South's long history of medical suffering—still, I couldn't help noticing during the 1960s, very much part of the lives of the Shortleys of the region, no small number of people, even today, and still a part, too, of the lives of Astor and Sulk and all their black kin. Hunger, malnutrition, illiteracy, a marginal economic existence, affect one's vision both literally and figuratively.

All that is rhetoric—the sociological ingredients of dozens of articles, aroused by reports, lengthy volumes. A storyteller with God on her mind knows that God is endangered by abstract formulations, by wordy announcements or exhortations. She does approach God's inscrutable presence through the South. But she approaches the South's many "social problems" through one woman's resort to them, it can be said, in her thinking. As that goes on (the mind's rush to fill holes before the fragile dam threatens to give way altogether) a moment of guarded hope arrives. The Shortleys' son fares well, when held up to comparison with the boy of the Guizacs. His name is H. C.; this Shortley is two decades along in his life, and significantly, he has his mother's "build." He also has trouble seeing; but rather than the ugliness of a cast, he has the burden only of glasses. If there is a tragic side to southern "poor white" life, scars irremediable and repellent, there is also another version of things—the solidity of a people able, sometimes, to dig in and last it all through. And their ability to get as much help as they can so that they can see as much as they can, given the bad luck they have come upon. H. C. "was going to Bible School," we are told, and, an American entrepreneur, he "was going to start him a church." Miss O'Connor knows not to overwhelm the reader with colloquial talk, cornpone talk as some might have it. She puts in that phrase, perhaps, because it is a wonderfully strong condensation of a personal and social purpose. The future pastor would be giving himself a start, as well as offering a building, a weekly (or daily) observance to others. Continuing in that vein, and offering us almost casually a one sentence summary of *The Protestant Ethic and the Spirit of Capitalism*, or closer to home, *Millhands and Preachers*, she lets us know about the following not especially incongruous characteristics: "He had a strong sweet voice for hymns and could sell anything."

Of course, nothing can be taken for granted, even one's better moments, even a comparatively good card dealt by those three fates, working away through the hours at their spinning. If H. C. has a fairly good future ahead of himself, it can be lost to someone's pushy avarice. As soon as Mrs. Shortley nods approvingly to herself, she has second thoughts. There is always a competitor, we all have learned—in rural Georgia, on Madison Avenue, of course, and it has to be added, within our academic enclaves. Just as someone writing about Flannery O'Connor counts nervously the number of books written on the same subject, and downheartedly gives up counting the number of published articles that address that writer's work, so it was that a Georgia mother began to eye suspiciously that priest who had taken it upon himself to bring the displaced person to this unlikely spot on God's acreage. She readily and with a surge of energy goes on the attack. She reminds herself that "these people don't have an advanced religion." And using indirect discourse, with a touch of country talk in it, the author gives us what she knows she could hear, any day of the week, any time of the day she chose, in Baldwin County, Georgia, among other places: "There was no telling what all they believed, since none of the foolishness had been reformed out of it." Such a line of reasoning gathers its own momentum. The next thought is a miracle of the suggestive; yet is as grimly concrete as a literary critic could wish, and is right out of the story—a quick repetition, in fact, of a previous image: "Again she saw the room piled high with bodies."

The camps of central Europe, the horror of Dachau and Buchenwald, have returned to the mind of a character in a short story, and obviously, to the reader's thoughts as well. And just in case we don't connect with a certain psychological inclination, Mrs. Shortley continues her scrutiny of this strangely attired and ominously broadminded man of God. She notices that he speaks "in a foreign way himself." There is "a throatful of hay" in his English—an ironic use of a familiar rural image to suggest something distant, unfriendly and suspect. And if his skin is blessedly white, there are other anatomical possibilities in him, in anyone, when the need is great: "He had a big nose and a bald rectangular face and head."

But the author is not quite done with her attempt to provide us, concretely and with the guile fiction enables, one of those "psychosocial contexts," one of those "sociocultural perspectives" we have grown accustomed to receiving in this century. She moves from the "psychology of prejudice" to the "sociology of aesthetics"—and, not incidentally, dips into a heady brew of religious symbolism. If one leaves the last out, for now, one is confronted by a sobering spectacle—a priest admiring a bird, one part of a country scene ("a tail full of suns"), whereas another "part" of that scene offers rather a different view: "Nothing but a peachicken." This divergence, serious and comic in its contribution to the story's unfolding, is meant to remind "us"—who, for example, buy books and read them and react to them appreciatively, as the priest does toward the peacock—that one person's joy is another person's object of indifference, or even, incredulity. All depending upon what? The intrinsic beauty of what has been regarded? The refinements of a particular sensibility? One's "socioeconomic background"?

The author has taken pains to put a bit of a squelch on any disposition we may have to grab hold of that last "factor." (Or is it "variable"?) She allows Mrs. McIntyre to tell us that she has no great love for peacocks, either. After all, they "scream in the middle of the night." They are being slowly permitted to "die off." If one person can't be bothered finding a certain kind of proximate beauty, and exclaiming its presence, another person has all she can do to stay asleep at night, without tolerating a source of constant awakening. She, too, has to keep her eye out for intruders—noisy threats to her night, which parallel the threats the Guizacs and their priest friend have collectively made to Mrs. Shortley's day. When one is thus assailed, one begins to take care of oneself as best one can. "The peacock stepped off toward the mulberry tree where the two Negroes were hiding," the authorial voice tells us, as the exchange about a given variety of birds comes to a close, and the action of the story proceeds. The Guizacs are driven to their "shack," where they are to settle in, and by their (intruding) presence continue to complicate a country life that the author in a few disarmingly plain and unaffected introductory passages has revealed as already complicated enough.

But the two blacks don't for long remain sequestered with the peacock under the mulberry tree—sharers in an author's symbolic recognition of transcendence, southern style. Astor and Sulk emerge, and with Mrs. Shortley engage in the first sustained conversation of the story. The author's command of her "social scene" is sure; and her humor, always a force to be reckoned with, is nowhere better. When, for instance, Mrs. Shortley is asked by Astor and Sulk who the new tenants are, she describes them as "Displaced Persons." She is then asked, "what do that mean?" Her response: "It means they ain't where they were born and there's nowhere for them to go—like if you was run out of here and wouldn't nobody have you." Continuing with this homespun existentialism, the author decides to show both Mrs. Shortley and the reader that even in the backwoods of a rural region there is the ever-present danger that the mind will get carried away with its own, didactic importance. "It seem like they here, though," one of the blacks points out. And he adds, now a teacher of the commonsense school, who wants to make sure he isn't in contention with an incipient logical positivist: "If they here, they somewhere." With a nod that Gabriel Marcel would have appreciated, the second black agrees: "Sho is." Then, he adds the assenting obvious, "they here."

We have been exposed in the tersest, least rhetorical manner to the often-mentioned stoicism of the South's black people—their capacity, born of their situation, to see exactly what is going on. There is no fancy mental footwork on their part. They come up with no clever rationalizations; no outbursts of anger, envy, resentment; no bitter asides that verge on the slanderous. What is must be acknowledged as just that—the resignation of someone who has been on the bottom all along, generation after generation, hence has no possible reason to feel threatened by a descent. One reason: the others, up there, can always come tumbling down, kicking out their bitterness, looking about keenly for someone, anyone, to scream at, assault. But Mrs. Shortley is hardly prepared for that kind of psychological analysis—a luxury for a lot of people who can barely get through a day, without suffering at the hands of various bossmen. "I don't think about anything," a white factory worker told me in Atlanta in 1964. Before I had time to come up with my inevitable (and privileged) "why," he had an explanation: "Once you start thinking too much, and wondering about this, and wondering about the next thing, you're on the road to trouble with a big T. Just look around you, and figure out what it's like, and act accordingly; that was my daddy's advice, and it's what I tell my kids—and myself, too."

Mrs. Shortley does think a lot, wonder incessantly about things. It may end up being the start of her salvation—but that is another matter. Whereas the blacks shrug their shoulders and keep their eyes and ears open and try to get by as best they can, and her own husband, as a matter of fact, does likewise, she goes around worrying and surmising and conjecturing and positing and extrapolating, and analyzing the thinking of others: "The illogic of Negro-thinking always irked Mrs. Shortley," the wry authorial commentator observes—a master stroke of irony, in view of the precise, earthy awareness the two black men have demonstrated. Through such a comment, and without the slightest evidence of an interest in any polemical tirade, the writer nevertheless barbs those who use words, ideas to construct their own kind of perceived reality, then resort to a quite special kind of denunciation—the intellectual's categories; for example, illogical thinking.

One person's logic can be another person's illogic, she knows and avers. It all depends on where one is coming from, and what one is looking for. Our capacity for objective logic need not be subdued by any moral system. Faith entails submitting our minds to a logic never firmly fathomable this side of heaven. One declares a faith only through the logic of one's own mind; it is everyone for himself or herself, as the blacks come close enough to reminding Mrs. Shortley—so that she becomes (the final refuge of the intellectual) moralistically pedagogical: "They ain't where they belong at." And having moved from phenomenology to exhortative hermeneutics, we are advanced next to the pleasures of hyperbole: "There's about ten million billion" displaced people waiting to cross frontiers, oceans, barriers of any kind, in order to find the smallest of destinies. Finally, there is the decisive, invariable regional fact of life—race; it is fitted into a conversation that reveals a lot more about the white side than the black. Mrs. Shortley has Mrs. McIntyre remark that "this is going to put the Fear of the Lord into those shiftless niggers!"

The two of them are, however, not at all impressed or taken aback. Whether it's actually been said or not, they've heard the slander before—again and again. It is not the Lord whom blacks have come to fear, but those who (the lament often goes) have stolen the world from the Lord. I owe that expression to a black Alabama tenant farmer. His general view of the intimidations of southern, rural life very much resembles the implicit line of reasoning Mrs. Shortley encounters as she tries on her various stratagems for size, and hopes, thereby, to knock down two blacks—but most of all, squelch her own formidable gnawing doubts and apprehensions: "I can tell how every white man and every white woman on God's earth is feeling. I take one look, and I know. It's up to us colored to figure the white people out; every morning we have to do that. Are they smiling, or are they looking in a bad mood? I know what's going to come out of their mouths before it does come out. I see the words in their eyes. I see the words on their foreheads. First it's the wrinkles, and then it's the eyes staring down at you, and then it's their big selves, trying to make small selves out of us. It's no good, but it's the life we've got, and there's no other for us here; and I don't think we do much better when we go up to Chicago, so we have to stay here and take what's been given us by the Lord.

"Jesus Christ, He didn't have it very good, either. So, who is the colored man to complain? Back when the Lord was here, there were those people who went after Him, and they didn't like Him none, *none*. They stole the world from Him. It was supposed to be *His* world, but they stole it. This isn't supposed to be our world. It's supposed to be everyone's world. But it's been stolen, if you ask me—stolen from the colored people, that's for sure. When you've been robbed of all you've got, you don't have a thing to lose, and all you can do is get up with the sun, and go to bed with the moon, and remind yourself, falling asleep, and waking up, that soon you'll be there with Him, and He'll be laughing with you, and there will be stories to swap. He's been where we've been; He's lost his world, and so have we. When the white folks start telling me I'd better watch my step, or I'll be in deep trouble, real deep trouble, I say to myself: something has gone wrong for them today, *for them*. They're right, I'd better mind myself—but it don't make any difference what I do; it's what happens to *them* that will make the difference. If the day gets better for them, they'll come around, smiling. If the day gets worse, they'll come around cussing. We know their ups, and we know their downs. We know the words that go with their ups, and the words that go with their downs. We know. And we know the words to use back."

For a writer who modestly kept to her own (racial) kind, so to speak, Flannery O'Connor did right well in conveying how a region's blacks feel, day in, day out; and just as important, learn to get on psychologically. The apparently offhand treatment she gives Astor and Sulk, the restraint she uses with respect to them—no effort to get inside them, no interest in offering them a chance to talk and talk, only the briefest description of the way they look or speak—don't prevent her from accomplishing a devastatingly accurate picture of a certain social scene. Sometimes what is portrayed as "superficial," turns out in knowing hands to be the deepest possible presentation of a particular set of circumstances. The surface of things has been, for many blacks, the only refuge they could find. When that set of customs and habits break down, there is fear as well as hope.

Without trying to speak for the likes of Sulk and Astor, but aware of how things go even as we prepare to enter the 1980s, among the rural sections of the South, I venture to offer a black farmer's view of "the changing South," with the reminder that Astor and Sulk weren't even *that* independent of the white world, since they were hired hands: "I'm not clapping my hands about 'freedom.' They's come, and they's gone, all the freedom people. We's left. We'll never go; we won't go North, and we won't go to Atlanta. When it changes here, we'll know; and it hasn't, no sir, not much. Still the same, really; it is. Lots of talk about us, I'm sure. Lots of changes in Atlanta, I'm sure. We can go vote. But so what! No difference in the day—or the night. Maybe a difference on voting day—some of us voting in the white man. Not enough of us here to do anything else! It's best when we keep quiet, and when they do, too. It's worst when we talk, and they do, too. Any time a colored man and a white man say a lot of words to each other, you know we're in trouble, us. The less we say, the less they say back, and the better off it'll be for everyone. If they don't like my idea, let them come show me what they plan to do for us—that's what I say to the people who tell us to raise our voices and start marching down the street. I marched. I was twenty and I marched. I'm forty, and it's all the same here, brother, it's all the same. No matter that they let us in the country courthouse now. So what! So what to the favors we got for ourselves! In my stomach, it's all the same! On my feet, it's all the same. I haven't moved out of here, and I can't, and I won't. No place for me to go. I know people who thought different, and they went, and they're back. No fooling. It's no fooling business."

How much "deeper," I have often wondered, can one go into the mind of such a person? How much more of the "reality" he lives with, and belongs to, can one justifiably evoke? Do we get nearer to a "psychological truth" if we claim for him words and emotions unexpressed —the "inner voice" of his mental associations—even though denied by him as part of his life? We have the right, some will say—the obligation, even—to help his ideas, his concerns, his "case," to be known. Why *not* speak for him—imagine what he has on his mind, expand the hints, the brief asides, he gives us, until the long frustrated eloquence of a whole person speaks through a fictional character?

That is a reasonable strategy for a novelist—but not the only approach to the black people of the Baldwin counties of a certain region. Do any whites, poor or not so poor, or quite well off, get any "deeper" psychological treatment from Miss O'Connor in her various short stories? Mrs. McIntyre certainly talks more, is more forthcoming about her views, her personal history—but so it goes in the world with her kind. Do we, thereby, listening to her, reading this account of her, get to know any "better," any "deeper" what goes on in her "deep-down" thoughts? *She* becomes in this ironic tale the displaced person; yet, for all her voluble self-pity, and nostalgia, and hard business sense, repeatedly given expression, she is not about to plunge into her soul, and come up with the kind of introspective self-scrutiny we might have hoped for, given the terrible crisis she witnesses, and really, distinctly shares in. Her noisy, self-serving prattle gives way, in the end, to a silence. She has joined the company of black people, whose cryptic rejoinders have so often interrupted long stretches of unutterable white sadness. We are told, in the end, that she lost her voice—a white addition to the voiceless blacks, the voiceless poor. This is not a storyteller who wants to find eloquence gratuitously—or insist upon it, for readers, when in fact it is not part of a world she knows rather well, and keeps trying to understand. The black people she constructs have their own way of trying to comprehend that world; and maybe, at the end, Mrs. McIntyre, who for the first time in her life has stopped talking or indulging her own thoughts, is preparing to join their (spiritual) company.

But, to return to the first hours of the displaced person's time at Mrs. McIntyre's farm: an important exchange takes place between the Shortleys. The wife goes to seek the husband out, tell him what she has seen—describe the nature of the intruding beast. Mr. Shortley is where she told the boss he was, in the barn, with the cows. There is a tender moment between the two, much needed, but not overdone. The author is signaling us, as with Astor and Sulk, that she isn't primarily a caricaturist. She has her ears open for funny exchanges between people, but she wants the Shortleys to be believable. He stares at her, she at him. He oughtn't to be smoking in the barn, but there he is, he has defied the boss by lighting up, and her reprimand to him is minimal. Why not sneak a smoke? Why not, especially, in view of what may be threatening to happen?

But the two of them are not really prepared to take seriously the possibility that a displaced person might make of them a displaced family. They laugh at the Guizacs, and so doing, show a certain kinship with the blacks. Better them than complete strangers. As for the priest, as an agent of the foreigners, he inspires a not unfamiliar anti-Catholicism. "I ain't going to have the Pope of Rome tell me how to run no dairy," says Mr. Shortley, who has been told that the man who arranged for the Guizacs to arrive can bring many others over. Taking that remark literally, Mrs. Shortley corrects her husband: "They ain't Eye-talians, they're Poles." A funny rejoinder, meant to show a certain parochialism—or on Mrs. Shortley's part, a failure to respond properly to her husband's more abstract mental life. Still, in that brief statement, a writer with a sure feel for southern dialect manages to anticipate a future president's early campaigning problems with pronounciation, and manages also to offer a historically humorous rejoinder, given the nationality of the present "Pope of Rome."

And so, in a matter of a few weeks "poor white trash and niggers" get lumped together by Mrs. McIntyre as "sorry people," and a writer has completed, in the first part of one story, a significant appraisal of a shared destiny. Now, relentlessly, the author goes after the person who makes that appraisal—using the foreigners, really, as a means of revealing a property owner's willful determination to save money, employ the most reliable, dependable, hard-working help. The author contrasts Mrs. McIntyre's moralistic apologias for what amounts to a greedy desire to get more for as little as possible, with the largely mute, long-suffering blacks and the perplexed, agitated whites, who are deeply offended by the shift of political balance on the farm. As the plot of the story unfolds, we begin to see the white South with a subtlety sociologists would find hard to evoke, at least with numbers or categorical terms. The Shortleys leave in a huff, and Mrs. Shortley dies. But before that happens the commercial crassness of Mrs. Mc-

Intyre is made clear—not in this instance, either, with the sledgehammer of authorial sarcasm or thinly disguised political and economic argument, but in the course of folksy conversation between Mrs. Shortley and her boss. "One fellow's misery is the other fellow's gain," says the increasingly triumphant Mrs. McIntyre, as she looks about her place satisfied at having, at least, someone desperate enough to work day and night—with an edge of zeal lacking in others, black and white alike.

The foreigner poses the threat of an altogether different set of values to a society that has managed to deal in its own way with issues of race, class, and sex. Guizac may be regarded as a Yankee industrialist of sorts, full of energy and determination, ready to work and work and work, as if his life itself depended on such an attitude. It turns out that he is as disruptive as any civil rights activist ever could be—more so, in fact. The rhythms of southern farm life depend upon a shared willingness, on the part of everyone, to accept all sorts of unexamined propositions. As the author makes clear, the blacks can be as shiftless as they can get away with being—a pitiable but necessary safety valve for people who get precious little for anything they do, no matter how strenuous. The whites are allowed to cut corners here, cheat there, and always, boss the blacks around, thereby assuaging *their* sense of loss or hurt. Mr. Shortley, we are told, has a still on the side, and he constantly sneaks his cigarettes—not allowed, supposedly, in a dairy. And Mrs. McIntyre herself turns out to be a woman who, at thirty, married a seventy-five-year-old man, thinking he was rich. He left her nothing, really, but the farm: yet another southerner, this time a white *woman*, who has been cheated by the manner in which a particular social scene ends up affecting its various members. The moral of all this is that there isn't much of anything for anyone, that the owner has been stranded, and her workers, of both races, barely manage—though, of course, the satisfactions and trials of race and class continue to make their presence felt.

But the essential fragility of those arrangements is revealed by what transpires in this story. Mrs. McIntyre's aged husband was a judge, and two of his "sayings" are oft repeated by his widow. The first, quoted above, seemed just right to justify the fateful arrival of the Guizacs. Europe's "misery" was to be Mrs. McIntyre's (the South's) "gain." On the other hand, that shrewd old judge had also declared that "the devil you know is better than the devil you don't," a conservative statement if ever there was one: the distrust of a rural society, with its strong sectional pride, for anything new. The entire story, it can be said, centers on that dilemma. If the South, so strongly rural even into the second half of the twentieth century (as Carl Degler persuasively argued in *Place Over Time*), is ever to change decisively, it has to take advantage of the amoral nature of a market economy, or so its political and business critics have told it. And those critics have not only been outsiders. Many who have urged a New South, have done so with fancy, dressed-up pieties that come down to the judge's opportunistic philosophy: take what you can get, and don't worry too much if what you get turns out to be the skin off someone else's back, because that's how the world goes, and tough luck for "them."

The agrarians, sensing the voracious greed, the endless materialism required to keep the fires of Western industry going, asked their fellow southerners to consider what they were, what they still significantly are, and to hesitate long and hard before exchanging their birthright for a cup of porridge—that is, one kind of evil, despite all the misery it prompts, for another kind, especially in view of its observable impact upon the world. Without having to preach a single official sentence of agrarianism, or strain anyone's credulity in the least, the author makes that point implicitly through the Polish displaced person, who is, after all, someone whose life has suffered at the hands of a "civilization," a modern industrialism, a Western, secular materialism gone viciously berserk—and now come South, full of promises, and ready to deliver immediate satisfactions: efficiency, reliability, productive mechanization, a kind of silent, impersonal competence and skill.

The South in the person of the middle-class, yet insecure Mrs. McIntyre says yes, yes indeed; but also hesitates. The tension builds as she becomes enamored of the displaced person. The threat of job loss triggers fear, sadness, suspicion, and rage in the Shortleys, especially the strong-minded and strong-willed Mrs. Shortley—the old, God-fearing, marginal (economically and socially) rural white South, which will not be easily displaced. She sees the nature of the threat, translates it into a biblical imagery thoroughly available and familiar to her, summons her family and insists that they leave, forthwith. The South will be invaded, will have to withdraw, but will never go crawling on its knees in surrender, or turn into a whore for Mammon. Anyway, that's the point of the New South; it is meant for city people —swinging lawyers and businessmen, and the college crowd who rationalize the ascendant commercial interests, or in the country, for judges and their wives, for propertied people who can make bucks and more bucks. Or so Mrs. Shortley, and not she alone, knew to think.

Her mind comes aflame with apocalyptic visions, and no doubt the author has an important biblical message for us, one which Robert Fitzgerald has immeasurably helped us realize in his essay "The Countryside and the True Country" (*Sewanee Review*, LXX, Summer, 1962). But in addition to the salvation of certain souls, the South and its often touted "special way of life" are at stake. Mrs. Shortley overheard her husband's boss contemplating his dismissal and that of the blacks. Mrs. McIntyre was afraid her displaced person might himself take up and go North. In one story, in the narrative construction of its scenes, we find a region's history given life: the fierce attachment of its laboring poor to the only land they know, the one life they can imagine; the alternative of departure—not embraced with enthusiasm and hope, but with a sense of resignation, of loss, of terrible foreboding; the mixture of affection and competitive truculence among the whites and the blacks, who know they must share the extremely limited benefits of a "scene" by no means ample in its earthly opportunities.

In a brilliant comic move, the author has Mrs. McIntyre learn that Mr. Guizac is arranging to get his young cousin over—by marrying her to one of the blacks: a foreigner thereby can enter the country. From that moment on, the story moves along to its tragic end. The New South has its price, is a mixed blessing, exacts punishment, suffering, and, maybe, turns out to be a dubious advantage indeed, for everyone concerned. When Mr. Shortley returns, a widower, we know one casualty of "social change." When he and Mrs. McIntyre stand paralyzed, watch the tractor, out of control, run over and kill Mr. Guizac, another casualty is recorded. Who is guilty? Of what? Those are theological questions—to be answered in Heaven or Hell, as the case may be. However, Mrs. Shortley knew of Satan's "stinking power" over us who have yet to meet our Maker or Judge. "Christ was just another D.P.," Mrs. McIntyre said contemptuously, as she tried to get her priest friend to pay attention to *her* ultimate concern—the farm and its caretakers. That giveaway line tells us, definitively, of the author's major interest—that we look at the South (we certainly shall) as a place where the enactment of religious drama connects with the everyday life of a people. But that life generates its own share of comedy, even if it is not divine in nature; and no small amount of tragedy. In the end only the priest visits the broken Mrs. McIntyre, whose greed and moment of murderous inertia (no raised voice to warn Guizac of impending doom) have taken their toll. Bedridden, she listens to explanations of the Church's "doctrines." No way to be saved! Yet, she is not completely alone; a black woman cares for her in the limbo of despair that is her remaining life.

It is no gratuitous information, that last fact, tucked into the author's last paragraph. Here is a southern writer drawing once more from a certain social scene in order to say something about it—as well as about Heaven or Hell: the blacks as custodians of God's charity, bestowed mysteriously and generously upon sinners. One last quote, in connection with this story, from a black Georgia woman, who for all the world might be that anonymous "colored woman" whom Flannery O'Connor describes as someone there "to wait on" the fallen Mrs. McIntyre: "I wait on them all the time; and I don't feel so bad, doing it. I feel sorry for them. Everyone feels sorry for us—I mean, everyone who comes here from the civil rights movement. They're right; we're not 'running our lives.' They tell us we should 'run our lives.' You know what? I'm running the white people's lives—the ones I wait on. They tell me they don't know what they'd do, if the Lord came and took me, and I hate to say it, because it sounds like I'm boasting real bad, but I pray to God that He spare me until the girl and the boy I wait on grow up, and then I won't feel too bad. I'm supposed to help the missus, but she says the kids need me more than she does, and if I help them, I'm helping her; and then, she'll call for me, to come and do her a favor, even if the kids need me; and it's back and forth, back and forth—until I'm dizzy. I'll be walking home, and I'll wonder who's free, and who's not free; and who's lucky and who's not lucky. I sure would love to have a little of what they've got, but I'll tell you something, they're not as well off as you might think. If you ask me, the Lord isn't smiling on them! He may not be smiling on us colored people, either; but I know he's checked them out, my white family, and shook his head, and said no about them. And I hope I'm not 'blaspheming,' like the minister says we shouldn't, but that's how I feel. My minister told me, I can take a look and say what I think, so long as I admit I'm only guessing. No one can ever really figure out what God has for His meaning."

Like a fellow citizen of hers, a one-time white resident of Milledgeville, a town a mere twenty miles away from her "place," this black woman, speaking those words in 1963, can't help going from "race relations" and sociology to theology. And like Flannery O'Connor, the black woman lingers with her senses on the daily circumstances she contends with: voices calling for her; the appearance of one or another person. She is not an apologist for any southern version of the *ancien régime*. She is *not* a woman Uncle Tom; never was. She can't, however, erase from her mind the ironies and ambiguities that press upon her all day, seven days a week—and no vacation at all: "none, never." She observes that the mighty are weak. She observes that the helpless offer enormous help to those so helpless they don't even recognize the extent of their need for help—the magnitude of the help they constantly expect and receive. She observes, in sum, a world; so did a contemporary of hers from Milledgeville. What Flannery O'Connor did in her story "The Displaced Person," as she pursued her main business of storytelling as a means of showing the depth of God's mysteries, was to ground the reader in the southern land, and draw upon its inhabitants knowingly, surely, suggestively, revealingly as recruits of sorts. The result is a series of reminders about God's earth as well as His universe, His commandments: a rare and an exceedingly high kind of sociology, history, social psychology.

Another of her stories, "Everything That Rises Must Converge," deserves mention here, especially because she herself, in her correspondence, referred to it as her one attempt to have a say on the vexing issue of race—and do so in the early 1960s, as a white resident of a small Georgia city. Her correspondence also registers her awareness of the not completely favorable reception that story received at the time; she suspected, in at least one case, that the reviewer might well have been a black person, or white civil rights activist, who misread her altogether. And I have to acknowledge the criticism I heard at the time; criticism I felt *rising*, to use that word, within myself. There they were, the black and white activists of the South, awakened by Rosa Parks and the tradition she came from (for many decades before the 1960s, certain blacks had fought, however great the odds, to assert their political dignity); and there we were, as readers—expected to remind ourselves *why* some whites (and they were few enough in those days) chose in favor of sitting beside a black person on a bus, or in a restaurant or moviehouse. What did Miss O'Connor have in mind when she gave us Julian: the use of psychology as a defense of the segregationist status quo? An ironic effort, it would have been, too—given her contempt for the manner in which America's twentieth-century culture so predominantly calls upon the social sciences in matters once thought to be ethical, if not religious in nature.

The story is considerably shorter than "The Displaced Person." The author wastes no time; in the first paragraph she alludes to the decidedly topical theme: "She would not ride the buses by herself at night since they had been integrated." "She" is Julian's mother, an obese woman, afflicted with high blood pressure, who has been told to lose twenty pounds or so. She has that one son, and in a page or two, we learn that he doesn't like her much—even though, or maybe, for the very reason that, she has worked and struggled to give him every advantage possible. Here, too, Christian history and symbolism are quickly worked into the narrative; Julian is "waiting like Saint Sebastian for the arrows to begin piercing him"—when, in fact, he is waiting for his mother to put on her hat, so they can go catch that fateful bus. But here, too, an earthy, concrete, unpretentious but exact and instructive social vision offers itself to us: "She was one of the few members of the Y reducing class who arrived in hat and gloves and who had a son who had been to college." And then comes more, the sum of it an approximation of a kind: the urban South of good dreams of yesteryear turned into a sour, cramped contemporary reality.

Miss O'Connor is not a writer who indulges the fantasies of her characters without discrimination. And she is never sentimental. Julian's mother, never given a name, always known as that, her son's surviving parent, is held under tight rein, though we can imagine what other writers (Tennessee Williams, Carson McCullers) would have wanted to do with such a person: reveries, spells of wistful memory, airs put on and put on, evoking tearful sympathy in the reader. But this writer is derisive, though with control. We get to know a woman canny if not calculating enough about the workings of class to forego a compassionate response from us. Still, she has pluck, force, and certainly opinions. And when she says that she "can be gracious to anybody," we are inclined to believe her. She then adds this as an explanation of why her manners are always correct: "I know who I am."

An unsettling assault on the cult of "identity"—one of those secular fads Miss O'Connor shrewdly kept her eyes on. There is nothing accidental about that line of discussion between mother and son. As the son comes to the obvious, realistic conclusions about the world as it is, the mother doesn't so much retreat into a dream world, or argue him down through her own, selective observations, as draw on history, and of course, psychology. Julian observes that many people wouldn't "give a damn for" his mother's graciousness, and that "knowing who you are is good for one generation only," and that right now she really doesn't know who she is. But she repeats that she does possess that knowledge, and he'd better emulate her: a sense of identity is the answer for one's personal life; a sense of identity will buffer one —enable a kind of inviolability, if not transcendence. No matter if things seem topsy-turvy, and there are many problems, even hard times, socially. One harks back; one keeps in mind what used to be—distinguished political ancestors, plantation owners, slaveowners and so on; and one does so in a way that has consequences for today; yesterday's achievements become everyday psychological bulwarks.

Julian will have no part of all that. He wants to be realistic, delights in pointing out the facts—a family's serious, pitiable decline. He has obvious scorn for his mother's racial condescension: "They should rise, yes, but on their own side of the fence." He also has to keep on facing her ironically, *au courant* psychology, constantly pushed. "The ones I feel sorry for," she announces, "are the ones that are half white." She adds, obviously the sensitive person, that "they're tragic." And she summons a virtue of our age, empathy: "Suppose we were half white. We would certainly have mixed feelings." That last expression, of course, is one more psychological banality of this century. Miss

O'Connor had read the autobiographical book by John Howard Griffin, *Black Like Me*—an effort of a white writer, through makeup, a tan, whatever, to live (he knew for only awhile) the life of a black person, and then tell others what he had experienced, in hope of arousing a compassionate identification. Miss O'Connor was not one for such efforts; she was skeptical about social psychology, and amused at what she considered to be a naïve gesture—a superficial rendering of a complicated regional life, one that is simplified only at a serious risk. And yet another example of the cult of "feeling," whereby anything that someone has "gone through" automatically assumes a certain "validity"—and more dangerous, possesses the larger authority of lending itself to social explanation.

No wonder the author has Julian fire back, sarcastically, that he has those "mixed feelings" at that very moment. In an earlier age he'd have dreamed of wringing his mother's neck. But he is also on his way to a significant complicity with her. The mother wants to talk about "something pleasant," and begins to remember the old days, the family mansion, the grandeur—architectural, culinary, as well as social. In no time the son gets swept up. He is his mother's son. When younger he had seen the place; out of necessity, it had been sold. Even then it was decaying. But he had dreamed of it as his mother had portrayed it. A child's dreams express not only conflict but an abiding loyalty—a testimony of a particular family life. Miss O'Connor doesn't have to get into the pedantic trap of saying any such thing. She simply narrates. She mixes memory with desire and taste. The present-day Julian recalls in his dreams the wide porch of the mansion, the high-ceilinged hall, the worn rugs and faded draperies. A mother's glimpse of a fading aristocracy, rendered concrete in a mansion, had become a child's vision of wonder, of a world lost, yet very much claimed, successively, in a second or two of one night, then another; and finally, had become a grown man's occasion for innocently revealing reflection. Julian observes to himself that "it was he, not she," who might really have understood the worth of that dying old mansion. Its quiet, fragile, necessarily understated appointments fitted in well with his disdain for the vulgar ostentation of the nouveau riche.

There he is, trapped in pride. We have been tempted to write off his mother as a stubborn but doomed woman; her resilience is interesting, her resourcefulness undeniable, her responsiveness to our contemporary life not as minimal as might be supposed by those who would want to read her as lost only in other, earlier illusions. But her son is no easy alternative to her. His illusions may be less apparent, less easily ridiculed, but they are there—and hard to take, perhaps, for many of us who read Miss O'Connor, and are glad to be known as tasteful, as appreciative of the "threadbare elegance" the writer conveys as Julian's notion of his ancestral heritage. He is pleased to think of himself as having been sensitive, as having noticed their reduced circumstances and wished for a better, *culturally* richer life—one worthy of his aesthetic refinement. His mother's will to survive, as an apologist for her might describe it, is regarded by Julian as an aspect of her "insensitivity." She thought otherwise, of course, and so doing, had recourse, yet again, to the language of our time: "being adjustable."

We are less than a quarter into the story, but the author has, in a sense, told all. Her intentions are revealed as ironic. She won't simply play off an old fool of a woman with a morally superior young son; a collapsing era of ignorance, exploitation, racism with a newly emerging period of egalitarianism, racial harmony, social intelligence; a South of blind resistance to change, enhanced by romantic delusions, with a South of awakening idealism, quickening progress in the direction of the old national mandate, so long fought, and fought off: "equal justice for all." And she won't set up those convenient polarities in the early 1960s, when they were craved by those who wanted not only political and economic and social changes—for the South, then, the one word *racial* summarized all the changes being sought—but, as a boost, maybe, some symbolic evidence, as well, that a revolution in sensibility was under way, a companion to the specific deeds being done, week after week, in country courthouses, restaurants, state buildings, city buildings, schoolhouses, not to mention buses.

As she notes in one of her letters, the Flannery O'Connor who wrote "Everything That Rises Must Converge" was the Flannery O'Connor who was also being urged to meet with James Baldwin—in Georgia. She refused to do so; up North, yes—but not at home, among the people she lived with, and whose struggle was, of course, her very own. She had a severe distrust of what every writer is tempted by, and in one way or another, no matter the resistance offered, falls victim to:

preaching. If she was going to tell others a few things, she wanted the message to emerge from the concrete particulars of her stories—a life evoked—rather than through public statements and signed editorials and television interviews. She was not averse to an essay, to a college lecture, to nonfiction as a mode of inquiry, but she wanted some congruence, some convergence even, between what she wrote as a storyteller and what she had to say on a college lecture series. And Baldwin had become a passing (it would turn out) hero of people she innately distrusted (more on that a bit further on): the northern liberal intellectuals. (He gives evidence himself, years afterward, of distrusting the very same people, though he would probably say, in retrospect, that he was playing a "role," and it was of some help, at the time, in bringing an issue to—how does the phrase go?—the "public consciousness.")

In May of 1964, under the duress of an accelerating civil rights movement, she would write: "If I had been one of them white ladies Griffin sat down by on the bus, I would have got up PDQ, preferring to sit by a genuine Negro." And in the same letter, to a southern friend who lived up North: "About the Negroes, the kind I don't like, is their philosophizing, prophesying, pontificating kind, the James Baldwin kind. Very ignorant, but never silent. Baldwin can tell us what it feels like to be a Negro in Harlem, but he tries to tell us everything else too." This is the voice of a Milledgeville, Georgia, woman who, like others white and reasonably well-to-do and in touch with national developments both racial and cultural (the two were decidedly connected then), felt a strong pressure being exerted: yield, change, and the quicker the better. Part of her knew that there would, indeed, have to be such a regional alteration of behavior. Dr. King earned from her no exclamations of approval, but she knew, and said that "he's at least doing what he can do and has to do," no mean concession for that moment in the South's history, the spring of 1964.

I mention the foregoing because it is important to understand the kind of pressure coming to bear not only on a region but a writer rather significantly in touch with a number of Yankees, or southerners become Yankees, none of whom come across as very conservative, or certainly, racist. What she set out to do was create a drama in a bus, a scene on wheels, a place where racial politics was coming to a head. She set the stage for that drama by showing us not a distinct polarity, but an illusion thereof. Actually, she spelled out some common ground—at a time when others were emphasizing who stood on what (*different*) ground. And worse, from the point of view of some civil rights activists at the time, she sneaks up on the reader, by setting the stage for a more conventionally "liberal" resolution of her story—because, even though Julian is his mother's son, and deep down shares some of her notions, not to mention her pride (a sin Miss O'Connor would hasten to emphasize that never discriminates—not by race, creed, class, national origin), he does for a while challenge her convincingly on her obviously outdated and narrow racial views. He makes sure that he sits beside blacks on the bus. He can't stand her patronizations, her justifications of the segregationist status quo, and lets her know that repeatedly. He cringes when she scans the bus, sees it half-filled with white people and says thereupon: "I see we have the bus to ourselves." And cringes again, no doubt, when his mother gets this response from another white woman: "For a change"—followed by: "I came on one the other day and they were thick as fleas—up front and all through."

But as quick as we are exposed to that line of conversation, we meet up with complications, they might be called—a blurring of distinctions. Now class mixes with race. The woman who has had a word or two with Julian's mother continues the conversation. From a person firmly rooted in the South's urban working class, we hear this: "What gets my goat is all those boys from good families stealing automobile tires. I told my boy, I said you may not be rich, but you been raised right and if I ever catch you in any such mess, they can send you on to the reformatory. Be exactly where you belong." Good advice. And advice that enables Julian's mother to announce that he has "finished college," that "he wants to write," but that instead he is "selling typewriters."

A devilish Miss O'Connor had herself a celebration; by the time she's through with the exchange, not at all extended, the ideals and aspirations of three whole classes of people have been exposed and satirized: the impoverished servants of an aristocracy; the working class; and the would-be intellectuals. Only then does the central action of this story begin: "a large Negro" boards the bus. The white woman with whom Julian's mother has been conversing moves away, because the black has had the nerve to take the opposite end of a seat she had been sitting on. Julian's mother makes a snide remark: "Now you see why I won't ride on these buses by myself." Julian joins the battle, takes the white woman's place. His mother is enraged. He is delighted at her reaction. He becomes even more provocative, asks the Negro for a light, in defiance of a No Smoking sign—and even though he has no cigarettes, hasn't smoked in months.

As the bus moves along, Julian dreams southern, white, liberal dreams—or parodies of them. Why not make friends with Negro doctors, Negro lawyers, Negro professors—"the better types?" He even imagines himself a civil rights activist, or bringing home "a beautiful suspiciously Negroid woman." The author stops short of caricature, but by now we know the motives behind such fantasies. This is a son, an only son, who is angry at his mother, but has never really (so far) been able to break away from her. A banal psychological situation becomes for Miss O'Connor an occasion of humor first (the exchanges between mother and son), followed by telltale daydreaming on the son's part. We (the integrationists, presumably the overwhelming majority of Miss O'Connor's readers) begin to feel quite uncomfortable, even before the rather swift climax of the story. Is the author connecting one of this century's clichés, an oedipus complex, with the South's racial crisis—as if to say: much ado about, well, not nothing, but something that is so drearily commonplace as to be unsurprising and inevitable?

Now a new pair come upon this bus, with its class and caste conflicts galore—a prickly black woman and her son, who (we soon learn) are not about to sit still and take it, take it: the once calm, compliant blacks of the Old South. The boy is restless, inquisitive, unbound, it seems, by conventions and rules, even those of his mother, who is, herself, a pretty tough customer. Julian is entranced. The woman who is first called colored, then, as her true (psychological) color emerges, a Negress, has on her head the same hat his mother is wearing. A delicious accident of fate. A handsome irony. He savors this fine moment, and expects the worst of his mother (shock and dismay), which would, of course, be the best possible outcome for him: his convictions about her once more confirmed. The New South is on the verge of yet another dramatic, perceiving triumph over the Old South. The author puts it succinctly: "Justice entitled him to laugh." This is an abstract, arrogant, snide "justice," and gradually Julian earns less and less favor from many of us: the small-minded liberal on race—a questionable improvement on the small-minded moderate or out-and-out segregationist.

At this point the story moves swiftly to its termination. The black child plays up to Julian's mother, who is only too happy at the prospect of basking in the old, familiar routines: white, parental benevolence, as against black, childlike submission. The Negress will have no part of that, however. As the bus pulls toward its final stop, so far as this story goes, Julian sees readily what his mother has in mind: a nickel for the dear, little one—the eternal southern "boy." She has no such thing to offer, however—only a penny. And there seems nothing he or anyone else can do to stop her. She makes the offer. The boy's mother explodes with the inflamed rage of her red pocketbook, which smashes the elderly lady down—where she sits dazed, silenced. The son gives her an integrationist lecture: no more sweet, pitiable bribes, in return for ingratiating passivity, surrender, subjection. But an era has ended in the South: the mother's stroke is silencing her forever, bringing such behavior to an end. And as that happens, Julian becomes a child whose mother is dying, a child who feels sad and not a little implicated in her death.

Needless to say, Julian is no unqualified hero. Some of his remarks are bold, perceptive, telling. I heard nothing from civil rights workers during the early 1960s that Julian, in one way or another, doesn't say or come close to saying. On the other hand, he has his weak, pretentious, hypocritical side. And as his mother lies on a city pavement, mute and shuddering before Death, and as a man becomes a child, some of us get upset and wonder at the author's intentions. An exposure of the infantile underside of such people—strong in dissent, but out of a truculent, neurotic intent? A slap at those who mind the business of others, while their own stables need a good deal of cleaning? A suggestion that the South needs change from some other quarter than it was receiving in the late 1950s and early 1960s—and therefore, one of those "psycho-social" commentaries, if not implicit indictments, we have come to accept as part of our proper fate?

Flannery O'Connor wrote this story shortly after the well-known civil rights incident in the Greensboro Five-and-Ten (1960). She wrote the story about five years after Rosa Parks started Montgomery, Alabama, and the entire South, down the road toward the integration of buses. She wrote the story well before the Mississippi Summer Project got underway—the critical turning point, with respect to the Deep South, of the civil rights movement. (She died as that project was proceeding.) She wrote the story in the rural South, before Milledgeville or other small Georgia cities had really come to terms with the everyday meaning of racial confrontation, never mind the changes it eventually would cause all over the region. It is not a story meant to celebrate much of anything. Had Miss O'Connor written a different kind of story; had she, to repeat, invited James Baldwin home, to Andalusia, or better, to her mother's stately antebellum residence in downtown Milledgeville, hard by the Governor's Mansion of the old Confederacy; and had she, as a final thrust, allowed television to show all of that "carrying-on" to the public—well, she'd have become a great heroine of the early 1960s to many of us, a pronoun from which I certainly don't exclude myself.

When Miss O'Connor wrote about Julian and his mother and the other white woman on the bus and the black man and the black mother and child, I was working in the office of the Student Non-Violent Coordinating Committee (SNCC) in Atlanta, and hearing a few "stories" myself from white youths and black youths. Some of what I heard was biographical, some autobiographical. Some of the remarks were strongly political or racial in nature, some quite personal, reflective. And there was humor as well as the grim combativeness one would expect from people taking chances, as a matter of fact, with their lives. One of the individuals I talked with longest, got to know best, was herself a white southerner—and so, part of a very small cadre within the movement: an Alabama woman whose skin color was white, whose "background" was upper middle class. She told me that there were "things" she hoped someone would be noticing and preparing to write about, in the interests of history. Her uncle was a professor of English with a strong sense of history, and she had heard him talk, in all too detached a manner (for her, at the time) about "the long run"; and yet, she wondered if there was not indeed a case to be made for such a point of view.

"I look around and hear people," she once observed, "and I wonder who has the truth." Then she steeled herself: "We can't let the South off the hook. The South will never change, if it's not pushed to change—pushed and pushed. Isn't that the lesson of history? On race, we've fought with guns and we've fought with laws and we've fought with deals, all kinds of deals. And we've dragged our feet, and waited—until the rest of the country got tired, and we could go back to 'our way.' Talk about 'the Southern character!'"

Then she relented a bit: "I don't know what we're like, but I know we're as mixed up as other people, all over the world. The only difference is that our troubles always get filtered through the race issue, because it's such a big part of our life down there. No matter who you are, and where you come from, and what's bothering you, there's always the white folks or the colored folks to reckon with! Right now, that's *all* we care about in the movement. But if we get through the next few years, and we change things down here—then, what will be left? Us! We'll be here—men and women and children: families—people getting in each other's way, or helping each other out, and every degree and combination of the two! Until my dying day, and my children's too, I guess we'll have a special feeling about race down here, even if we win every civil rights battle we fight. It's part of our *life* here, race; to Northerners, it's a problem—a problem down here, and one up there. But for us, it's the way you live—with your neighbors. The time will come when I won't be a civil rights volunteer any more—the sooner the better. And then we'll have to face ourselves, I guess. I shouldn't talk like that! I shouldn't look ahead more than a day. Do today's work today. Too much thinking about the future—and you stop doing your best in the present! But somebody has to think about the future. The historians think about the past. We're trying to change the present. Who thinks about the future?"

The novelist. A writer such as Flannery O'Connor, who was already inclined by temperament and outlook, and disposed by the nature of her craft, to do what that fellow southerner of hers mentioned—spell out what race fits into, is but one element of (no matter how substantial the magnitude). Writing in the early 1960s, Flannery O'Connor chose to draw upon a preoccupation of the time: who will sit beside whom on a bus. But she knew that any public spectacle of that kind is but an extremely brief expression of a longer, larger drama. She was not, after all, a publicist; nor was she a journalist—a profession by no means without considerable importance and, Lord knows, value, when a struggling, oppressed minority tries to break free. Nor was she without compassion. Nor was she a segregationist. Nor was she, really, to use language we used to use in SNCC all the time, a member of the "power structure." No Rotarian or Optimist in Georgia, no amoral "old order" in the South, or alas, the equally amoral "order" that so often gets called "the New South," will find any comfort in her stories, or her two novels.

In "Everything That Rises Must Converge," she demonstrates, again, her interest in the sin of pride. No discussion of her work can leave out its major religious themes, approached constantly in both her fiction and nonfiction. And the South, for her, as was everything in this world, for her, turns out to be a part of God's world—not the Georgia governor's, the American president's, or that of the Chamber of Commerce, the Klan, the civil rights movement. But what does she tell us in this story about integration? She tells us that whites can be silly, frivolous, stupidly fearful, riddled through and through with petty thoughts, absurd daydreams, and prone to exaggerated self-regard. She tells us that avowed segregationists can talk nonsense and think they are in touch with the realities around them. She tells us that a man who is reasonably well educated, reasonably intelligent, and possessed of reasonably sensible views about what is right and wrong can, at the same time, succumb to meanness, spite, his own version of exaggerated self-regard. She tells us that skin color is a particular way that people set one off from another, but that even in the segregated South, where such a "factor" is paramount, there is a lot more to say—a lot more involved than the sum of any "social" factors (were it possible to quantify the matter) could possibly indicate. She tells us that integration in the South is an occasion for people to learn not only about one another, but about themselves. She tells us, not least, that integration in the South was something needed as desperately by white people as blacks—and as desperately by those whites who paid it lip service as by those whites who opposed it vehemently or with a restrained moodiness.

She tells us that when the buses are integrated (and everything else once segregated, too) there will be no new Jerusalem of a South, only people who are fairly decent, and people who are rather indecent, and all measure in between. And she more than hints that she is talking about both races; she has no interest in sparing blacks the burdens (but to her theological mind, the dignity) that go with being a sinful human being. The black mother, one suspects, isn't only a victim of the thoughtless, self-centered, callous white world—though a strong case for such a characterization of that world was made, one must keep emphasizing, and made in a manner that lasts with the reader: the difference between yet another preachy editorial, and the insinuating provocations of well-constructed fiction. The black mother, we are told right off, is not only "gaily dressed," but "sullen-looking." She is that before she gets on the bus, a description that precedes or supersedes the action described—her ascension, if such it is, to an integrated bus.

We might want to say that she was sullen because she apprehended all too clearly her immediate future, and so doing, fell into despair, while struggling against despair. I fear the author would scoff at such an interpretative leap. She would reserve the right to describe someone's temperament as a given, for that person, so far as the story goes. She would expect, of course, a rejoinder: even if the woman is, generally, glum or sullen, there is a reason for such a state of mind—her race, her experience of rejection, discrimination, and so on. Whereupon the author would think of all the sad, dreary white people, some rather well off, she has known in "real life"; and of the few she has tried to approximate fictionally.

There is something presumptuous and shallow about consigning people to the unqualified imperatives of psychology and sociology. A person can be sullen, for instance, because she is exceptionally knowing, has looked hard inward, has had a bad *day*, not life; because she is chronically ill with a disease unconnected to race, class, sex; because she had a fight with someone, a fight that has to do with love, rather than hate, jealousy rather than envy, or to quote the obvious phrase, pride rather than prejudice. Miss O'Connor wasn't writing a novel, and so she hadn't the space, given her limited intentions, to render an account of what went into the sullen appearance of the black boy Carver's mother. But she was fiercely reprimanding, whereas another black mother, equally outraged by the stupidity of Julian's mother, might be differently upset and corrective toward her child. (There is the suggestion that the black child, Carver, already has a touch of Julian in him—a rebelliousness, a determination to break free of all too obvious, maternal constraints.) This is a story, though, of the privileged white world: so full of itself, all possessed of the power and the glory, and so much in need of coming off its high horse. And who better to write that story than someone not at all a stranger to that horse and its various riders?

Flannery O'Connor's South is Robert Frost's New England, is Sarah Orne Jewett's Maine, is the artist-storyteller Frederic Remington's cowboy-and-Indian West—American regionalism in the service of a vision that glances toward Heaven and Hell, both. And she would, correctly, want added: Hawthorne's Concord, rather than that of Emerson, Thoreau, and the Alcotts. Even as the New England romancer, Hawthorne, turned his back on the secular humanism of the eighteenth century, in favor of the religious intensity of the Puritan divines, she had no great hopes for "big, bustling Atlanta," as we used to hear it called in the early 1960s: "a city too busy to hate"—another slogan much used then as the ultimate, commercial justification for integration. Her view of the South is both protective and critical. She obviously was proud of her homeland and not only aware of its special qualities, but anxious to make clear her debt to a people and a tradition: the land, the talk, the habits, a whole way of seeing and doing alike. The essays in *Mystery and Manners* are formal in nature; they were, mostly, college speeches—rather more carefully prepared than those of others who move from college to college, taking the place of preachers. But despite her restrained and occasionally severe comments, she could become warmly personal about a place she felt very much part of, glad to call her own. Her reliance upon her region is clearly stated in the essay "The Catholic Novelist in the Protestant South." At one point, straddling psychology and sociology, and in important respects casting both aside, she observes: "The novelist is concerned with the mystery of personality, and you cannot say much that is significant about this mystery unless the characters you create exist with the marks of a believable society about them."

Mystery is something not "resolved," as today's "complexes" are, by something called an "interpretation." Mystery: something that *is*, something that one learns to behold, appreciate, respond to, rejoice in, turn towards with tears. The "marks" of a society are not labels, and descriptive categories, and generalizations heaped on generalizations, in turn heaped on anyone and everyone in sight. Marks are traces of the world, each uniquely a certain person's—worked into the face, the tongue, the gait, the vision of the mind's eye, the hearing of the mind's ear. She goes on to say tersely, emphatically, "The image of the South in all its complexity is so powerful in us that it is a force which has to be encountered and engaged. The writer must wrestle with it, like Jacob with the angel, until he has extracted a blessing." Those are, quite obviously, fighting words; they are the words of someone bound and determined not to become a regional celebrant, apologist, or for that matter, critic. They are the words of a novelist who saw the temptations of dialect and ritual and history itself; instead of using them selectively one surrenders to them, and so doing, becomes as narrow and stereotypic, after a fashion, as the faddists who come boasting of other territorial (literal and figurative) affiliations: the "perspectives" of social science; the latest act in Manhattan's unceasing melodrama.

The author of "The Displaced Person" wants a lot from Georgia: but she knew that she had to keep a close eye on that Georgia, that southern scene, lest it become an occasion for a story with the title, "The Displaced Person Comes South," or "The Georgia D.P." And, if "Everything That Rises Must Converge" did indeed take place in Atlanta, say, rather than Boston or Chicago, it is nevertheless a story whose titular action by no stretch of the imagination belongs exclusively to the American South. The upward movement on that bus—a white rising to steer clear of a black, an older son rising to defy his mother, a son's anger rising, a black woman's combative arm rising, a white woman's hopes rising and falling and rising and falling, as she remembers, anticipates, listens, watches—is indeed southern. But it partakes, as well, of what Teilhard de Chardin, Jesuit biologist and theologian, had in mind: a movement maybe best described in the phrase "slouching toward Jerusalem," the city on the hill.

Flannery O'Connor's correspondence, even more than the nonfiction she crafted into pungent essays, offers many references to the South. In the more relaxed vein of letter-writing she was able to risk more of her strong opinions, and tell more of her story, so to speak. Indeed, the correspondence is so rich and crowded with ideas, personal statements, accounts of what has happened or is about to happen, that the reader goes through the six hundred pages as if in the presence of a novel: Miss O'Connor, a particular human being of strong, idiosyncratic voice, and Miss O'Connor, a southerner, a Georgia woman of the mid–twentieth century. On the subject of the South she is as outspoken as she is in her essays. At times she gets wry, detached about the region. At other times she is ready to fight with any weapons at her disposal against various adversaries, imagined or real. In an early (1954) letter to an admiring critic she observes: "Since you show an interest in the book I presume you are a foreigner, as nobody in Georgia shows much interest." She even goes further: "Southern people don't know anything about the literature of the South unless they have gone to Northern colleges or to some of the conscious places like Vanderbilt or Sewanee or W & L." She turned out to be wrong; her correspondent was a Georgian. And maybe she was a bit harsh on her fellow southerners; it ought to be noted, right here, that she was looking, looking, always looking: at the South's poor; at the South's talk; at the South's various citizens, including its writers—and that (there or elsewhere) she pays them heed.

She was always listening. When an unknown admirer sent her a giant azalea bush (1957), she was delighted for her mother, who loved azaleas. But the mother already had in mind a somewhat similar gift for Miss O'Connor, who reported on the following exchange between Regina Cline O'Connor and one of the blacks who worked for her: "They were planting it and she said, 'Be careful with that now, I've given it to Miss Mary Flannery for Christmas.' 'This ole bush?' he said. 'It's a very nice bush,' she said. 'She yo only chile,' he said, 'and you ain't going to give her nothing but this ole bush?'" And she was unable to miss a southern irony: the Klan abandoning fiery crosses in favor of electric bulbs; the Klan riding about in motorcades, and "distributing baskets to the needy." She was also unable to ignore a northern insult, not all that unusual in nature: "My mother and I were amused (startled) to read in Mr. F. W. Duppee's letter in *Perspectives* that I lived in an unlikely sounding place called Milledgeville where my mother raised hogs and I raised peacocks. My mother can't stand pigs and has never allowed one on the place—but now she is raising them it seems in French, German and Italian."

What is one to do with the ignorance and bias implied in such a Yankee misstatement, or lapse, or whatever? Milledgeville is no more "an unlikely sounding place" than Manhattan, Manhasset, or Massachusetts. And to bring in hogs—a pure fantasy, a pure fabrication—is to reveal unwittingly what parochialism can do, even to a distinguished literary critic and English professor who taught for a long while in a university located in an unlikely sounding New York City place called Morningside Heights. Miss O'Connor alternated between annoyance and the humorous reaction she mentions in the face of such patronizing Yankee comments. Mostly, she kept her cool and directed her perceptive energy to the nearby scene, letting the North and its important people take care of themselves. She was constantly attentive to the people who worked at Andalusia: "There ain't a thang wrong with daddy but two things, heart trouble and asmer"—a statement of a man helping at the farm, and a statement worked into a letter because the writer saw what those words conveyed: irony, forbearance, stubbornness, an ability to mock one's suffering condition, however serious.

She was constantly keeping track of the black people who worked for her mother, especially Shot, whose comic tribulations, as he tried to get an automobile license, are reported to various correspondents. At one point (in 1957) she makes a comment that would, understandably, have offended certain readers then, not to mention now: "Noblesse obleege with a vengeance as my momma runs it but very peaceful. They are the only colored people around here with a white secretary and chauffer."

A Yankee has a right to upbraid a writer who is quick to point out the condescension that gets sent down from Morningside Heights, and fails to point out the Milledgeville variety. No doubt the blacks did keep Mrs. O'Connor on her toes. She drove them to doctors, to stores; she ran interference for them before various officials. She mediated their (sometimes rather vicious) arguments. She worried about them, taught them, encouraged them, exhorted them, and not least, shared her thoughts and sentiments with them. Miss O'Connor isn't one to glorify that state of affairs, or apologize for it, either. She finds, yet again, an irony or two: who is bossing whom around? In the clutch, however, the white South has always bossed the black South, and the appearance of the contrary, however interesting, can't be taken too seriously. Hence the humorous nature of the comment—and the shrewd juxtaposition of "noblesse obleege" and "vengeance." Even though the latter is often used precisely as Miss O'Connor does, and with no intention of suggesting specific hostility, let alone revenge, there is a double edge to the use here. The author adds, after all, "but very peaceful." There is a lot of smoldering resentment on both sides —plenty of feet dragging, much grinding of teeth as the importuning takes place in sugary language. All that going on every day, and probably not at intervals, but constantly: submission, provocation, command, obedience, disobedience, and we learn, a touch of deflected vengeance—the drunken excesses of farm help. Nothing to be proud of—black and white. I think the comment, with its parody of a French expression, bespeaks nervousness and shame—and a determination not to yield too much (then, at least) to those two emotions: the rural South in the late 1950s, deteriorating and on the brink of a social explosion.

In 1958 she wrote to a fellow southerner who had gone North that there was for Georgia "a choice of three segregationists: 1) The present lieutenant governor whose only visible merit is good looks; 2) A hillbilly singer, Leroy The Boy Abernathy; and 3) A rabid preacher who claims to be backed by the Bible." Then, in jest, and ironic reversal, she expresses her disgust: "You live in the wrong place, girl, but I done told you before." Her obvious disgust is tempered by a mixture of wry amusement, and maybe, a reluctance to turn on a part of the South in a letter addressed to a friend who had chosen to say goodbye to the region, and in fact, scold it from afar for its obvious flaws. There is, of course, a tradition for that—southerners who have left for a mixture of personal reasons and out of conviction, and who become steadfast critics of their former homeland; even as there is another tradition—the Yankee who goes South, not as an (self-righteous) evangelist, but for his or her own (escapist) reasons, and ends up an apologist for the new homeland, or less emphatically, quite fond of it, hence willing to overlook its faults.

Miss O'Connor herself had left home in pursuit of a career: the Iowa

Writer's Workshop, thence Yadoo, and finally an important time, both personally and professionally, with Sally and Robert Fitzgerald and their young, expanding family in the Connecticut countryside. Disseminated lupus erythematosus, a disease whose name she herself must have appreciated, put an end to an exile never meant as a reproach to the South. She went home sick; eventually was spared death for a number of years by the emergence of cortisone as a palliative in the so-called collagen diseases, of which lupus is one; but through an active correspondence, a perusal of general magazines, literary quarterlies, and newspapers, occasional trips to campuses and to see friends and publishing people in New York, and toward the end of her life, through television, she kept in touch with the nation as a whole. At times she could be obviously critical of both the white and black people of the South. But let an outsider take after the region, even if the person was a good friend, and a sharp, even caustic way with words was soon being mobilized in defense.

In her unguarded moments, however, when she didn't feel the accusing finger of people themselves walking on precarious moral territory, she could, with a word, a phrase, indicate the complexity of her attitude toward the South: "It is great to be at home in a region, even this one" (1959). At another point, she cannily and sarcastically makes this observation: "I have a friend who predicts that the school crisis in Georgia will take the following course: the issue will come to a head, the Governor will close all the schools, the people will realize that this means no more collegiate football and will force him to open them again." And with her refusal to see Baldwin on home turf (1959) went some important indications of her essential attitude toward the racial issue, not to mention a clue about the way she regarded the relationship between herself and her neighbors: "No, I can't see James Baldwin in Georgia. It would cause the greatest trouble and disturbance and disunion. In New York it would be nice to meet him; here it would not. I observe the traditions of the people I feed on—it's only fair. Might as well expect a mule to fly as me to see James Baldwin in Georgia. I have read one of his stories and it was a good one. I am just back from Vanderbilt and have had enough of writers for a while, black or white." It is possible, with good reason, to take strong issue with those last remarks—though, Lord knows, anyone who argues with them in

1979 or 1980 and fails to consider what it was like in rural Georgia at the time the author wrote that letter, is taking one of the serious risks that go with retrospective historical (and moral) analysis.

She was constantly noticing what happened around her, mindful of a need to ground her imagination in the concrete truths of a particular region. Let others, with their symbolic flights of fancy, make a big fuss over the life she portrays. One student, for instance, asked her (1959) why the Misfit, a character in "A Good Man Is Hard to Find," wore a *black* hat. Her reply: "I said most countrymen in Georgia wore black hats." She adds that the youth "looked pretty disappointed," but was undaunted. "Then he said, 'Miss O'Connor, the Misfit represents Christ, does he not?' 'He does not,' I said. He looked crushed. 'Well, Miss O'Connor,' he said, 'what is the significance of the Misfit's hat?' I said it was to cover his head; and after that he left me alone."

She was impatient with more than Nashville writers. She resisted all conclusive sociological categorizations—efforts to subdue the complexity of human experience through words such as *race, creed, region, ethnicity, sex, age, occupation*. But she had a keen eye for those qualities of mind and heart that engaged themselves with the world around her. And she maintained a blunt interest in racial matters, and issues of class. She corrected the dialect in stories written by her friends. She told them what she had observed—a lot: how blacks felt about the comparative lightness or blackness of their own skin color; how various white southern people referred to their children; where blacks live and don't live in Georgia; who is above or below whom socially, culturally. She had a harder and harder time, as she became better known, making those observations discreetly. She began to attract a fairly unrepresentative crowd—by mail, and sometimes, alas, in person: the nearby ones who read her, and God forbid, became caught up, personally, in the fiction she produced.

"Anyway, my mail for the last two weeks has been from rural Georgia," she commented in a note to a friend toward the end of 1959. She continued with examples: "Letter from a man in Macon who wants to buy two Chinese geese, letter from a girl in Jonesboro who has an idea for a musical comedy based on the Civil War but is 'not versed in literary type writing' and would like me to write it for her, letter from a carpenter in Thomaston ('i seen the pece in paper about you') who would like to send me his picture, letter from lady in Toccoa enclosing three tracts of Oral Roberts and a magazine called *Healing* (crutches in picture)." And thereafter, tersely: "All these letters are from people I might have made up."

A year later, she observes that "some very odd people turn up hereabouts, usually hoping to find me as unconventional as themselves. However, as I am highly conventional, most of them go away." She was sensible enough not to get swept up by such attention, or to lose sight of who was regarding her closely, and why. She saw how funny and sad and strange and even bizarre—yes, grotesque—some of her region's "good country people" could be. And no doubt about it, she didn't need them knocking on her door, or filling up her mailbox; she had taken long looks, and got to know well the various rhythms, messages, displays of belief and habit. Perhaps she worried, as she implied in her remarks about Baldwin, that she was exploiting a scene's eccentrics for her own purpose as a writer. If so, she knew it was what writers do—knew, one might say, that it was her manner of struggling with and losing to the Devil, while also tricking him once or twice.

Yet, if she was hard on herself for deliberately emphasizing what she knew to be the strange side of southern life—from the point of view of *southerners*—she was even harder on those who used her writing to confirm outrageously ignorant prejudices. It is a successful southern writer's fate, often enough, to have to endure celebrity for the wrong reasons—a form of notoriety, in fact: that *strange* Flannery O'Connor, from that *peculiar* rural Georgia, offering up these (wonderfully, unnervingly, gruesomely, horribly—depending upon the reader's taste) outlandish characters. The misreading of her work, the associated misapprehension of the South, was not confined to this country, needless to say. "I'm obliged for the clipping from TLS," she wrote to her publisher, devoted friend and admirer, Robert Giroux in late 1960. "The only British review," she added, "I have seen that you haven't sent me was one by Kingsley Amis in *The Observer*. It was extremely unfavorable but he ended up saying that I had convinced him that this is the way people were in Georgia. (Horrors!)"

It took precious little convincing, she knew. In a number of high and mighty realms, Georgia's subtleties and complexities—social, racial, religious, cultural—are not exactly appreciated or celebrated. It is all madness or decay, rotting fluted columns belonging to abandoned plantation houses, or blacks in chains and flogged constantly, or whites fluctuating, with respect to their intelligence, between a level suitable for the designation of idiocy, and a level applicable to morons, and maybe, if lucky, within the "low average" range. "The Sahara of the Bozarts" the honorable H. L. Mencken said, and as Miss Mary Flannery might have said it in one of her letters, slipping as she did into a defiant localist posture, there ain't nobody who's forgot what the guy said about us, and tough luck for them, because if they want to keep on being no count fools in what they think, then that's their bidnis and no one else's.

Meanwhile, she could only keep her cool, endure the ignorance of others, be pleased with a lessening of the ignorance she knew to be near at hand (and to exist everywhere, in various forms). "I guess you are reading about how we are integrated now in our educated part," she observed wryly to a northern-living southern friend in early 1961. Then she moved to a more general observation: "There is a marked change of atmosphere about all this in Georgia. They are fixing to junk the segregation laws and substitute a more local arrangement. Don't think now we will repeat New Orleans." How right she was—and at a time when others, who prided themselves upon their savvy as political analysts, were full of grave doubts—some based on an inclination to regard southerners as inherently lawless, violent, unpredictable and mean-spirited. She was, no doubt, herself going through the changes she accurately saw taking place in her home state. All the while she fought lupus—rather as segregationists fought their enemies: both losing battles.

She was for Kennedy against Nixon. She placed herself politically in between CORE and the Young Republicans for Goldwater, a shrewdly stated polarity, perceptive indeed about a supposed transformation of southern life, the emergence of a two-party system. She traveled through the region, settled on New Orleans as her favorite city—if she ever were to live in a southern city. She scorned the efforts of Yankee magazines to understand her homeland ("I wouldn't believe anything the *Atlantic* prints about the South.") She would have no part of the (superficial, she thought) cultural modernism that went with the New South—the swinging early 1960s climate of Atlanta: "I have been right disgusted with all the sentimentality wasted on those teachers who were giving Steinbeck and Hersey to the 9th grade so I am writing on that. Ralph McGill had an idiot column on it in which he implied that Hersey was much better than Hawthorne." She took to reading the agrarians, reading C. Vann Woodward with considerable admiration. ("Southern history usually gives me a pain, but this man knows how to write English.") She watched the stock car races with excitement. She watched "the sportscast every day." She followed her unpopularity with the Atlanta newspapers—"those lying Atlanta papers," they were called at the time by our neighbors in Cobb County and surely by the people of Baldwin County. ("Did you see their mention of 'Everything that Rises Must Converge?' Unsigned. I suspect somebody from Atlanta U. did it.")

She watched integration begin to come (in late 1963) to Milledgeville with no alarm whatsoever. She wrote pungent, succinct political comments. After President Kennedy's assassination she noted that "a certain variety of Southern politics is at a standstill because now there's nobody to hate. Bobby no longer fills the bill and it's going to be hard for Southerners to hate Johnson." She teased her northern, liberal intellectual correspondents with wonderful asides, such as, with respect to her "state of being," that "it ain't much but I'm able to take nourishment and participate in a few Klan rallies." And she never missed a chance to get exactly at the center of things, as they were in her beloved South. In March of 1964 she was ailing badly—her last bout, it would turn out—with lupus. In the hospital, where she had an operation, her ears were always alert. She observed, referring to a nurse, that "her favorite grammatical construction was 'it were.'" And then, ever concrete, O'Connor adds: "She said she treated everybody alike whether it were a person with money or a black nigger. She told me all about the low life in Wilkinson County." The patient, in pain, laughed and laughed. If she'd been given years more to live, that kind of "low life," so much more of the South's life, "low" and otherwise, would have found itself realized—shrewd, funny, startling elements of a fiction which, sadly, has been denied us.

And maybe some of that fiction would have been a sensitive, knowing writer's enlargement, for her readers, of a scene she mentions in late March of 1964: "Yesterday we went to the doctor's office—same scene as in 'Revelation' but nobody in there but us and two old countrymen—about 6 ft. tall and skin and bones in overalls. They just had a talk. The first one said, 'Six months from now this here room will be half full of niggers.' 'Aw,' says the other one, 'it ain't the niggers so much. It's them high officials. Jest take the money away from them high officials and you won't have no trouble. All it is is money.'"

There weren't too many more letters for her to write after that one. Her story "Revelation" was, as the title implies, a primarily religious one—though, like the two we've discussed here, also full of carefully conceived and suggestive sleights of hand meant to tell us about the workings of race and class in the South. She was hurting badly in that doctor's office. Her body was under the helpful but dizzying, exhausting sway of cortisone steroids. The lupus-wolf in her had mounted its most ferocious assault. Yet, she was able to see (she was given by grace to see) a vision of her own—a revelation to match that of just about any other writer who has tried to analyze the South. She had glimpsed a still alive rural populism, all too long tucked under the bruised, hurt, inflamed white skin of countless men and women. Toward the end of her life she knew she had reached a watershed of sorts as a certain kind of writer. What she could do, she did brilliantly. She had been mining not only her mysterious gifts, but the existing "social scene" of the South (without embarrassment, she repeatedly acknowledged). That scene, however, had been slowly changing during the last few years of her life. Everything was, as Dr. Martin Luther King often put it, "under continual challenge," and with increasing success. It is a pity that Flannery O'Connor didn't live long enough to accept that challenge as hers—to use it in the making of various written occasions which surely would have offered all of us (wherever we live and come from and feel part of) wise words, sharp images, broad angles of vision, comic moments, tough probes: a storyteller's revelatory grace become incarnate.

TWO

HARD, HARD RELIGION

IN SEPTEMBER OF 1959 Flannery O'Connor wrote a long and serious letter to her friend, the novelist John Hawkes. Addressing herself as well as him, she made this statement: "I don't think you should write something as long as a novel around anything that is not of the gravest concern to you and everybody else and for me this is always the conflict between an attraction for the Holy and the disbelief in it that we breathe in with the air of the times." In the same rather long paragraph, she becomes less personally admonishing, more sociological: "The religion of the South is a do-it-yourself religion, something which I as a Catholic find painful and touching and grimly comic. It's full of unconscious pride that lands them [the people of the region] in all sorts of ridiculous predicaments. They have nothing to correct their practical heresies and so they work them out dramatically. If this were merely comic to me, it would be no good, but I accept the same fundamental doctrines of sin and redemption and judgment that they do."

She knew that the disbelief she referred to was no longer confined to certain sections of Boston, New York, Chicago, San Francisco. When we lived in Mississippi, then in rural Georgia, we were always hearing that New Orleans was "a city of sin," or "a cancer upon the South"; and that Atlanta was a "northern-bought city," or one-third more tersely, "Yankee owned." For Miss O'Connor, too, such a state of affairs was no cause for joy: "The anguish that most of us have observed for some time now has been caused not by the fact that the South is alienated from the rest of the country, but by the fact that it is not alienated enough, that every day we are getting more and more like the rest of the country, that we are being forced out not only of our many sins, but of our few virtues." For her one of those virtues was the "attraction for the Holy," she mentioned. And in the rural South, even today, that virtue is still to be found: *hard, hard religion*.

I got the phrase from one of those utterly impoverished white farm hands Miss O'Connor knew so well—a redneck, he'd probably be called. Miss O'Connor was herself, alas, not beyond the expression *white trash*, which I suppose would apply to this tall, lanky, leather-skinned, stooped man who several times raised not one but two hands high in the air as he delivered himself of a fierce, unrelenting jeremiad:

I wake up, and I remind myself that this isn't *my* day; this day belongs to God. I tell my children they have to learn about God in small ways. Sunday is one day of the week, but there are six other days, and the people who take themselves to Church on Sunday, and forget God all the other days are hitch-hiking their way to Hell, and that's that. My boy, I hear him say his prayers at night, and I remind him in the morning that he'd better start the day with a prayer, because prayer isn't only meant to get God's ear, so He'll forgive you for what you've gone and done; prayer is meant to get God's heart, and it's meant for Him to listen, and clue you in—tell you to be careful, or you'll be in a big heap of trouble, the rate you're going. I feel good when I'm on my knees, just out of bed, and I'm letting Him know what's ahead. Oh, Lord, I say, it's your day, and I'll try to meet you the best I can, halfway I hope. It's your sun and it's your sky. It's your rain and it's your wind. The clouds, they're sent over us by you. And I could go on and tell about more of God's miracles!

My oldest daughter said to me once: "Daddy, what about the worms, and what about the drought, and what about the flies and the mosquitoes?" I told her: Mary, you mustn't divide up the Kingdom, good from bad—what you like and what you want, from what you don't like and what you don't want. God put us here to test us, and there's no escaping Him, and there's no getting away from His test. If He wanted us all to get by, without a test, and stay near Him, there wouldn't be this earth, like we know it. The snake came, and Adam and Eve couldn't stay away from that snake; it got to them, that's what happened, it just got to them. Every day there's a snake in our lives; every day, I tell you. It don't matter who you are. It don't matter where you live. Your heart cheats. Your eyes cheat. Your ears pick up all the gossip in the town, and they won't let go of it. Those flies, they're inside us—landing all over the place. Same with the mosquitoes. There's nothing so bad on the outside, that it don't have its equal on the inside. I hear your mother bad-mouthing someone, and I know there's a lot of mosquitoes, a lot of flies that have got to her. And to me: I see some people in trouble, and I'll be a fly and land on them.

I'm not a hawk, just a fly, looking out for myself! My brother is a hawk; he'll go after someone, and he'll want to kill, I swear he does. They used to call me Timid Joe, a scaredy cat. No more; I've got me in some fights and won. But I'm no hawk. I'm just a bad soul, trying to get as good as possible, before I'm called. I'd hate to be judged today, this very day. It would be Hell for me, a long time of it, for sure. But if you pray, if you keep God close to you, and try to let Him guide you, every day, every week, "all the years of your life," like the minister says, then you are trying and He'll notice, He will, and you're in the running. A lot of people, they're wanting an easy drive up there to Heaven, that's what. They think they can go to Church on Sundays, and strike a bargain with Him. They think an hour or two on Sunday, or around Christmas and Easter, and when they die, they'll see a sign, and it'll say: Heaven, and the Lord will be yonder, on the hill, waiting, with a smile on His face. That's soft religion; that's faking. It's no good religion. It's a waste of time. Our religion is hard; it's a hard, hard religion. We're in trouble, and we may not get where we want to be going, but we're going to try, oh are we! We're drinking the milk fresh, every day, and it's sweet—praying to Him always, and that's what we're here to do, and if only we keep at it, there'll be a reward. Down the road it'll be. We'll walk up to Him, and we'll be tired, the feet will hurt, and we'll wish we could just stop and rest—and that's it: He'll tell us to sit ourselves down, and it'll be a long rest, brother, I'll tell you.

This man's words have been tampered with; but not much. Remarks made over a number of days have been pulled together, thinned out a bit, given the structure of sentences, and even some grammatical form. But a man's strong, earnest *laboring* religion still comes across, I believe; and his continuing sense of mystery; and the manners he takes care to mention, and render in detail, and suggest as necessary for his children, for all of us—creatures of God. The man has never read any of Flannery O'Connor's writing; he has never heard of her. He is unlettered, but he is the kind of person who taught her a good deal, and helped her find a way of being as serious, as "gravely concerned," as she most assuredly was.

The man is out there on his own, "doing his time with the Lord," as he put it. I found the expression a little too interesting, I fear. Did he mean to say that praying was very much a kind of imprisonment? "No, Sir," he let me know, right off. Then silence, a long one; I began to worry that I'd made a bad mistake bringing up the subject—my own self-centeredness, if not the sin of pride in full display: see what I say, see what I know, see how clever I am, and please cooperate, so that we'll both agree on that score—my astute interpretation now become our shared declaration of what constitutes an element of reality! Finally, he let me have it:

We're all in prison, all the time: we're sinners—here by the grace of God. This life is our one and only chance, our last chance, *the* chance God has given us. When we die, we either stay in prison, or we're sprung. No one knows who goes where; only God does. You can't get to Him with money. You can't get to Him by telling Him you're Mr. Big, and you have more money than anyone can count in the Citizens and Southern Bank. You can't get to Him by saying you've got all the education there is, and all the respect of everyone in the world. I'll say this, even: you can't get to Him because you're a farmer, or a lawyer, or a hired hand, or driving a truck, and if you're white or if you're black, that's not what's going to make God choose you. It's between you and Him—your soul, and what He's found out about it. That's why we're here—to be found out! There's no other reason. Sooner people knew that, better off they'd be.

I hear a plane up there, and I think of God. Is He going to come like that, and fetch me up? Flying saucers—you know what they may be: Him, coming for someone, and forgetting to cover his tracks. It's up to Him if He does forget; maybe He *wants* us to see a little of Him! I'm not one to know; I just pray, and leave the knowing up to Him. But we have these people who want to be able to tell me and you and everyone what's going on. It don't mean they'll ever be able to do that, though. You can only do what you're made to do. The Lord didn't make any of us out to be Almighty God. You can always fool your neighbor. You can always fool yourself. You can't fool God. And He never does play tricks. We're the ones who do that; we play tricks and tricks. He waits. He watches—and He counts. If I knew all the arithmetic in the whole, wide world, I still wouldn't know enough to count like He does. Keeping track of sin, keeping track of everyone's sins—that's the biggest job of counting that ever was. My wife thinks it just comes natural to Him; but I see Him sweating a little over those big numbers. Of course, it's not for us to know that much about Him. It's for Him to know all there is to know about us, and then there's the reckoning, just as there always has to be. You're alone when you face Him. This is a hard life, and that meeting is a hard, hard one.

All the time he and others I've worked with stand naked and fearful before their Creator. And as Miss O'Connor suggests, the result is a kind of personal torment; at times the result can also be a relentless self-examination that rivals the moral scrupulosity of some of the Catholic Church's religious orders, and surpasses, easily, the secular efforts in that direction by some of us in psychiatry. The psychological "mechanisms of defense" that enable a good number of nonbelievers to avoid any truly thorough, hard look inward are, as Miss O'Connor suggests, painfully, touchingly, sometimes comically absent in a person such as the one just quoted. He can tear himself open—not because he is a masochist, but because he believes he has God's mandate to do so. Those who have found Hazel Motes's driven, unyielding, determination strange or bizarre ought walk down some southern country roads, on any day or night, not just Sunday: Gospel music, and outspoken confessions, and petitions stated loud and clear, and thanks offered with cries and sighs and ominous, lasting, utterly intense silences. The fervor: a passion committed to God. His felt presence: here, there, everywhere—say those who claim to have Him nearby and right above and, not least, inside.

And the pride Miss O'Connor mentions, it is another constant presence of sorts. In her stories zealotry is pride; prophesy is pride; aberrancy is pride; robbery and murder and just about any mischief possible boil down to pride. She is not so much antipsychological (there is a touch of that, too—out of intellectual conviction) as she is disinterested in the psychology of her characters—in the psychology, one hastens to add, that this century has found to be so revealing and important. She takes for granted what the rest of us begin and end with; she forsakes the nervous rivalries and envies, the amorous or truculent intentions that many of us expect everyone, including our novelists, to explore—in favor of an examination of the sin of sins, pride. She does not do that scrutiny by resort to psychiatric reductionism. She parodies in several of her characters (Rayber in *The Violent Bear It Away*, Sheppard in "The Lame Shall Enter First") those of us who may be tempted to "explain" in psychiatric formulations what, for her, and for the yeoman farmer quoted above, is something irreducible—a given: God's will become man's fate, of which anyone's "psychology" is a part.

When Miss O'Connor refers in a letter to the "practical heresies" which the ordinary southerners she observed tend to enact in their daily lives, she is describing what she herself has tried to enact in her stories ("Parker's Back," for instance). But she is telling her correspondent, rather obviously, how a particular element in a regional life has connected so wondrously with one writer's natural endowment. An element, she makes clear, that is a pervasive religious one.

An element that has to do with the "doctrines" she also refers to—man's sinful nature, yet his redemptive possibilities, under God's watchful eye. Specifically, in her two novels, as well as in stories such as "Parker's Back" or "Good Country People" or "The Artificial Nigger," she is at pains to render a kind of religion she had, after her own fashion, studied rather closely: a backwoods fundamentalism that can be passionately idiosyncratic, constantly centrifugal with respect to any kind of institutional Christianity, let alone the hierarchical, solidly established Church Universal. Often that religion is a "blood" (instinctive) religion that paradoxically denies "blood" in favor of ascetism; a vehemently assertive religion, unafraid to articulate the triumphant violence in human beings, indeed anxious to be heir to that violence, so to speak: "Think not that I am come to send peace on earth: I come not to send peace, but a sword" (Matthew 10:34). It is, of course, precisely those aspects of southern religion, incorporated into the novels *Wise Blood* and *The Violent Bear It Away* that have made them so difficult for the twentieth-century secular humanists, they might be called, no matter their avowed faith, who have read and criticized her work—and sometimes, praised it, she felt, for the wrong reasons.

A substantial part of the literary criticism devoted to her writing, inescapably and properly, centers on the religious symbolism she uses; indeed, provides the reader in abundance. She knows her Old Testament and her New Testament, and she draws upon both explicitly—possessive, demanding prophets, suffering figures who seem sent from on high to perplex us, divide us one from another, and part of ourselves from other parts. But above all she was a theologically sophisticated Roman Catholic, as her essays in *Mystery and Manners* had told us; as her more recently published correspondence makes even more clear—the range and depth of reading she did in philosophy, theology, and not least, the religious story or novel. She was especially taken with those two French Catholic giants of this century, François Mauriac and Georges Bernanos. In a sense, she became, inevitably, a judge, far more compassionate and tender than she has been given credit, of her religiously wayward brethren. They are kin to her not only as southerners, as people from, say, Baldwin County, Georgia; they are kin, too, as Christians, obsessed as she was, as Christ told all of us to be—with Him, with what His strange and historically unique Arrival meant: God become man, the Word become flesh, the Incarnation.

Her God was the God who entered history, lived the life, came to know sin: "My God, my God, why hast thou forsaken me?" She knew the heresies her neighbors more than flirted with; she saw the theatrical side to their emotionally intense God-possessed days and nights. She saw in Baldwin County, every week, a series of miracle plays and morality plays, a parade of spectacles—sometimes part of, literally, a road company: the itinerant minister and his tragicomic presentations. Though she was a sophisticated, highly educated, and thoroughly rational person, she never succumbed to an arrogance that would have had her turn the South's "old-time religion" into a big joke for "them" up there, the northern cognoscenti, or nearer at hand, those belonging to the South's secular salons. She manifestly cared for her neighbors, was even awed by their fervent, searching journey toward Him. I believe her fiction to be a respectful portrayal and a loving reprimand. She was quite ready to welcome Pope John XXIII—though, Lord knows, she had no use for the heresies she saw her *Catholic* brethren more than flirting with: religion as sentiment; religion as secular ritual; religion as political instrument; religion as an excuse for communal assembly—a touch of neighborly affection on a day when one doesn't go to work.

When my wife and I were reading *Wise Blood* as carefully as we knew how, we were also going to one revival meeting after another, one public baptism after another, one evangelical assembly after another: in rural Georgia; in the mountain country of Appalachia; in the mission churches that "fed" the extremely marginal people of the South: migrants, the urban derelict, the far-out rural folk of the remote hollows of western North Carolina, eastern Tennessee, eastern Kentucky and West Virginia. We took rather more time than we should have to connect what this exceptionally, penetratingly concrete storyteller had to offer and what we were being insistently given as the Lord's truth in the course of our daily work. True, we were always being reminded, on the roads, that "The Wages of Sin is Death," that "Christ is Coming: Beware," that we'd better "Get Right With God—Or Else!" But what has that to do with Flannery O'Connor and Hazel

Motes or Tarwater, with Hulga and the Misfit and Mr. Head and his grandson Nelson, with O. E. Parker and his wife Sarah Ruth Cates Parker?

One evening, in South Carolina's high country, outside the hamlet of Tigerville, just south of the North Carolina state line, and not too far from the Georgia state line, we stood in a warm early spring evening, under a sky choked with stars, and heard the Gospel preached, heard some testifying, and heard music soaring toward the Lord's presence—the stars signaling back "Oh, yes," we began to think, caught up in the excitement. White faces: Celts, Saxons, an occasional Nordic streak, and maybe some French Huguenot ancestry. Poor people: farm hands; store help; truck drivers; gas station people; a deputy sheriff, conspicuously in uniform—there for awhile, then off in a roar, his red light, for all we knew, alerted by one of Pontius Pilate's emissaries. The preacher talked and he talked, quietly at first, then higher, then sweet and low, then so high it seemed a miracle that those small vocal cords in that larynx could generate so much thunder.

We expected the graves to open, the rocks to be torn asunder. We looked up at the sky, ordered to do so by the speaker, and thought that maybe those stars were forming some pattern, after all—a tatoo, or series of them, in need only of a few more words, so that their overall message would be revealed: we the obediahs (worshippers of Jehovah) are soon to meet Elihu (whose God is He). "Go ye therefore and teach all nations," the young towheaded man with hazel eyes and the thinnest of faces shouted. And continuing: "Baptizing them in the name of the Father, and of the Son, and of the Holy Ghost." Silence. My wife turned to me and said she wondered if O. E. Parker's wife was nearby. Knowing smile from me: two smart ones, glad to recognize each other, amid this ever-increasing Hell and brimstone. The voice continued: "Teaching them to observe all things whatsoever I have commanded you: and, lo, I am with you always, even unto the end of the world." Pause. Shouts of Amen. The preacher waiting. Will he say Amen? What will he do next? An Amen from him—followed by singing: his, alone, at first!

A terrible voice, a croak—but the face upward, in the direction of those stars. And soon, a return to Matthew, the twentieth verse, we later realized: "For the Kingdom of heaven is like unto a man that is an householder, which went out early in the morning to hire laborers into his vineyard." And more. Why that story? It goes on and on. The stars seem to fade. A wind comes up, but no earthquake. Time to go? We can't: too near the speaker. Next time we'll know better! And then that voice again. The groan becomes a cry, an exclamation, an insistence, a command—all of them eerily mixed. The voice is strident, plaintive, vulnerable, primitive, clever: "I will give unto this last, even as unto thee. Is it not lawful for me to do what I will with mine own? Is thine eye evil, because I am good? So the last shall be first, and the first last: for many be called, but few chosen."

Now the sky seemed precarious. Would the stars fall, be strewn about—jewelry to be picked up and worn by these self-declared as the "last?" Over and over they shouted to one another: "We're the last!" My wife and I were waiting for the earth to open. We were heretics of our own prideful kind; we toyed with the idea of our dramatic rescue—the Devil as Savior! Meanwhile, the affirmation of insignificance became so boastful that we wondered who would dare acknowledge any kind of social ascent ever after? Levelers all! Leveled all! The minister screamed louder and louder: "Let us avoid the priests and the scribes, the principalties and powers, the Empire, the god Mammon. Let us pray here that God is with us, that God welcomes us." And more. And enthusiastic assent. And then, the call for those who want to be born again; for those who have sinned, and want to confess their sins; for those lowly ones, those utterly humble ones, who hoped to follow, ever after, the "Almighty God," follow Him into Jerusalem, follow Him unto the end of time—when the stars and the moon and the sun and the planets all come together: "When everything rises up and meets the Creator, the living God of Eternity." Not quite rising, that "everything," to converge—we thought later, finally homeward bound in the secular sense of the expression.

Two days later we talked with the evangelist. He had repeated his anguished, confident, demanding, suggestive performance the night before. We had stayed in Greenville, reading one of those motel Bibles, more caught up in his zeal and touching charisma than we may have wanted to realize. When we met, he seemed, close up, a late adolescent, so thin we wondered whether he was sick. Yet, the emaciated body was topped by a strangely solid if thin head, long hair, and again, a powerful voice, even when carrying on ordinary, face-to-face conversation. He had been tough with his listeners, quoting to them from the twelfth verse of Matthew: "O generation of vipers, how can ye, being evil, speak good things?" We wondered whether he, in fact, felt those hungry, searching, acquiescent, thoroughly humble and hard-working people who came to see him and hear him so attentively were members of such a "generation." We wondered if the South's plain people, its ordinary farm people, living at the edge of things, never able to take much for granted, deserved such a harsh, accusing assault. We wondered that, out loud, with him—a bit more tactfully than I just indicated. Patiently, surely, with no embarrassment or apology, he let us know what the central issues were, and how far away we were from grasping them—until, at last, we began to understand that for him, if not for Flannery O'Connor, we were Raybers, Sheppards, citizens of Taulkinham: people across "a great divide."

He kept using that expression, and his explanation of things, of himself and his listening people, helped us understand Miss O'Connor's intentions as a writer. The people she gives us in both of her novels are kin to this evangelist, as well as others we came to know—individuals with a sense of mission that can be frightening to a spiritual stranger, as the small-time evangelist we happened to be hearing that day quite evidently knew:

> When I speak, I try to keep John the Baptist in mind, and what Jesus told us about him. John was the last of the prophets; he knew what was coming. Some of us may know, too. But are we really ready to believe? "Verily I say unto you, among them that are born of women, there hath not risen a greater than John the Baptist: notwithstanding he that is least in the Kingdom of heaven is greater then he." That was Christ, telling them, telling us, that no matter how good you are, and how big and important you are, and how much you know, and how much you think you know, it don't make the difference you might think. Even John the Baptist, who foresaw Jesus, and what He was going to mean to us—even he wasn't a disciple, a believer. He saw the coming of Jesus, but to us is given the highest privilege—not to see and understand and predict, but to follow through faith, to accept our Lord, who is here and waiting.
>
> A lot of people, they're like St. John, and Christ knew that: they try to figure out what's coming. You have your weather forecast people, and the astrologers; you have people telling you about what's going to happen to the planets and the sun; you have the people writing about the future of everything; you

have the people in the colleges, telling you how the earth came, from the gases, and how it'll end, one day, and having ideas about all that will happen between now and then. It's not fair to compare all these people to St. John the Baptist, because he wasn't denying Christ, he was just saying that you have to know where John's ministry ends, and where His began—the difference between a prophet and God, if you ask me. And that's a big difference, and there's a bad danger, preaching: you take your message so seriously, you forget in whose name you're giving it!

Now John wasn't, like the Book says, "a reed shaken with the wind." There were all those reeds, but he was different. He said what he thought, and believed; and if he went against the wind, then so be it! And he wasn't one of those people "clothed in soft raiment," the types who "wear soft clothing [and] are in kings' houses." He went to prison for what he believed. He didn't stick with the rich and powerful, and tell them what they wanted to hear. They'd have given him some right good clothes, if he'd just gone along with them. He wouldn't take their bribes. I'll tell you, if you have some leadership in you, there's always someone ready to bribe you. And the people will follow; that's where they're wrong. They haven't got the faith of Christ in them, not as completely inside as it ought to be. They'll settle for any old leader. They'll listen to someone, and lose faith. It's a danger we all face. That's why Christ said: "But what went ye out for to see? A prophet? Yea, I say unto you, and more than a prophet." There's this great divide, you see, between the old prophets and Jesus—and between Jesus and all the people who aren't believers and followers of His, but people setting themselves up as prophets, with *their* voice the main thing. You see what I mean?

We were beginning to see. There he was, drawing upon Matthew 11: 12; and there we were, confronted with a "great divide"—between him and us, between northern intellectual life and his southern, rural, evangelical ministry, and not least, between our sense of the mediating, if not redemptive power of institutional life, and his steadfast personalist convictions:

Anyone who really believes in Christ believes in Him in spite of the whole world, and what it says. There's no room, in Christ's world, for the man who says he's on the top of the ladder, and who says I'm the best, and you're not as good as I am. There's no room for the one who says he's gone to college and he'll give you the whole scoop, and he'll even interpret Jesus. Jesus interpreted Himself; that's what the Bible is. Jesus said that no matter how smart you are, if you believe in yourself, and not Him, then you're not headed for His Kingdom; that's that! So, the least shall be the most, and the bottom shall go to the top, and even St. John the Baptist, who was a prophet, was on the other side of the great divide.

You can cross over the divide—it's been done: from the Old Testament to the New Testament, from Rome to Nazareth, from the Pharisee Saul to Paul. You can cross over because of faith, and I'll tell you something, and it's hard to tell people this: you don't think your way to faith, and you don't buy your way to faith, and you don't get your faith by winning a race with your neighbors and your friends. Faith is a gift; it's God's gift. And who did He go seeking? The lame, the blind, the deaf, the sick, the poor, the prisoners, the people out of their minds, the people all the other people looked down upon. So, it's by His grace, that we're saved. It's in our blood to be damned. How do we know what we're made of? How do we find out where we're going? We stop; we look; we listen—and we pray. Come Jesus, come to us here, smile on us, lead us. Isn't that the way? It's not through college, and not through being head of the police, or the bank. And it's not through me. Anyone who preaches the Gospel is in the same boat as the people who come to hear. We're all sinners; and only He can save us, and I hope and pray He can save me, and you, and everyone—but it won't be easy, and the struggle was and it is and it will always be like it says: "From the days of John the Baptist until now the Kingdom of heaven has suffered violence, and the violent take it by force."

Silence. He seemed sure that we understood what he had just told us. But we were confused. We were not the thoroughgoing, exegetical readers our evangelist friend was. Not that he went to school to study the Bible. He disdained schools and colleges, as much as he disdained churches, ordained ministers—and priests, certainly. As for rabbis, he'd never met one. Nor was he a student of history or culture. He had attended high school, but had not graduated. He was a self-styled "South Carolina poor boy"—a son of a white farmer who had "gone to the mills," then become sick and died young, at forty-four, of cancer. The disease "took him in a couple of months." The man refused any and all medical help: Christ was calling him, and best to go. If He thought otherwise, He'd make His intentions clear. The world is full of "violence toward God," the father told his son on the deathbed, and the son had better always be ready to cross that "great divide," with hopes of being on God's side. That is to say, there is a continuing battle, with the enemies of Jesus scoring their victories constantly. Christ came prepared to fight as well as preach; and anyone who follows Him is, forget it not, a soldier. And the old man soon died, urging the son to fight fire with fire, to be a "loyal soldier," to be prepared for enemies everywhere, and to be prepared to die engaging them in battle: "The violent bear it away," not the meek and mild and moderate, not the ever so well adjusted and well educated and well-to-do—but again, the fiercely loyal, willing to live and die by a certain kind of sword.

Without ever having heard of Flannery O'Connor, never mind her second novel, this evangelist gave us a big boost in understanding what she was about—what her second novel was saying. Right off, one scans the title and wonders: bear *what* away? And why the need for violence? And can't we be more temperate, controlled, rational, tolerant? Of course not, any southerner who knows his or her Gospel religion, will tell you, and tell you again. Baptism: an acknowledgment of an apocalyptic change in the world, a violent break with the old order. Now one can take nothing for granted. Now descent from Abraham is not to the point—an entire privileged group banished. Now it is anyone and everyone who is eligible. Listen, hear God's Message—the Good News. No one is ineligible—not the poor, not the rebuked, not the scorned.

And those who are on top, who think they have certain rights, obligations, privileges by virtue of books read, capital accumulated, lineage of one sort or another inherited, had best know how radically, violently egalitarian this message, this story, this mandate, this personal remonstrance of our Savior was meant to be. After all, He shunned buildings and Pharisees, and talked directly to individuals, in the open air, upon hills and in valleys, near the water and along the dry, dry roads. "Come unto me all ye that labor," He said—as direct and inviting an "approach" as one can make. Not come unto my friends and agents and employees, as the evangelist kept reminding his listeners in the various sermons we heard. Each of those listeners, in his or her (predominantly) blue collar, casual clothing, during those weekly warm evenings, was told again and again that he or she stood there alone with God. The evangelist hoped and prayed that he had helped them pick up a sword, helped them lose their quiet, show-me neutrality, their easygoing Sunday avowals—in exchange for, yes, a madness for Him, an absolute conviction about Him, an obsession for Him, a compulsion to do His work. And if others say: mentally certifiable—well, the lines are drawn. It is a "harsh and dreadful life," as Dorothy Day, quoting Dostoievski, has never stopped saying these past fifty years since her conversion.

But that was a conversion to a Church, the Holy Roman Catholic

Church. And Flannery O'Connor, of that Church, can't help being a judge of sorts, in that Church's tradition. She knew what that evangelist was like, would have appreciated his theological errors—but also responded to his sincerity; and no doubt about it, would have shared much of his urgency with respect to the Christian message—thereby (with him) coming into a clear confrontation with our secular culture, which can readily appreciate, even elevate, other obsessions and compulsions, while regarding as grotesque the Christian kind. The world of sex manuals, of Masters and Johnson, of *Playboy* and *Penthouse* and *Viva*; the world of talk, talk, talk, about me, me, me; the world of military hardware, of hydrogen missiles, dozens and dozens, stored all over—such worlds are all regarded as part of a quite normal person's life. But let a Tarwater or a Hazel Motes or an O. E. Parker or a Misfit come on the scene, and we wonder quite seriously about not only them ("grotesque"), but their quite "strange" creator—whose obvious, emphatic talent compels us to get rid of her the best way we can: a rustic genius, full of primitive preoccupations that are the property of a culture that has a long way to go until it's on a par with ours, even if we all do share a common nationality.

Not that the Catholic Church is a stranger to the North, to New York, Boston, Chicago, and the West Coast. St. Patrick's Cathedral is not far from a few Manhattan literary salons. There is a Catholic Church right in the heart of the Harvard University dormitories. Why the difficult time had even by Catholic critics, writing for Catholic magazines, when it came to her fiction? She was not surprised; she knew that the Catholic Church was not completely immune to the tides of history—maybe less vulnerable than some institutions, but in the end, a victim nonetheless: prey to the very forces evangelists in the South rail against. The "practical heresies" she referred to are the quite natural hazards that get in the way of would-be believers. While we lived and worked in the South, we saw those heresies worked out "dramatically," as Flannery O'Connor suggested they get to be. We lacked what she possessed in abundance, a basis in our believing life to spot them instantly and appraise them fully. The experiences we were having with southern "hard, hard religion," however, and a continuing exposure to her fiction provided, at last, some sense of what those "practical heresies" were grounded in: a given kind of life.

What do the various heresies have in common: the Manichaean heresy, the Marcionite heresy, the Albigensian heresy, Jansenism—and not least, the Gnostic heresy? Gnosticism is an important element of the southern and Appalachian rural evangelical religion (and its urban, untamed offshoots) I have witnessed and tried to describe (in several of the *Children of Crisis* volumes). A continuing contention, that southern evangelist mentioned above would say, did say, has kept on saying, between the spirit and the flesh:

> A week ago a woman came up to me and confessed her sins. She said she wanted to stay here, and be loyal to Jesus, until He called her. But meanwhile, wasn't there some way she could get some help with her "bad thoughts?" I told her she wasn't praying hard enough. If you're a hard-praying person, Jesus will hear you, after awhile, and He'll take care of your troubles. He'll heal you. The flesh is an excuse; we can overcome the flesh. We can lick anything through prayer. It can't only be *me* praying; it has to be each sinner, standing there before his Maker: telling all, and hoping for Him to come and make a difference. He's the one who can make a difference; He's the one who can fix the push of the flesh, so it doesn't push us to sin.

In those small-town "assemblies," black or white, or up the hollows in those "open-air meetings," one sees and hears people trying to come to terms with their lives, to figure out the eternal questions that transcend race and class and nationality and educational background. Where do we come from? How ought one live this life? Where, if indeed anywhere, are we headed? Christ's prophetic voice answered those questions for His followers. He was one of a number of preachers who appeared on the scene some two thousand years ago—individuals whose words were hungrily accepted by people confused, uncertain, gravely worried. A great empire was showing signs of deterioration. A great and persuasive religion had, for many, become a hardened, rigid body of rules and regulations, the property of an austere, removed elite. Among those at the edge, among the marginal, there was little reason to pay allegiance to Rome; and even for many Jews, never mind the many non-Jews of what we now call the Middle East, a declining Hellenism and a seriously troubled Judaism offered little hope. Such a collapsing world was ripe, indeed, for messianic figures; and if many appeared, we now know that one truly prevailed.

But how that happened—that is, how a man of obscure origins eventually became regarded as the Messiah, became a collectively venerated, worshipped figure, is a story historians and theologians and archaeologists still struggle to unfold; in Albert Schweitzer's phrase: a "quest for the historical Jesus." And beyond that, a quest for the institutional origins of contemporary Christianity.

Christ addressed his most prominent disciple, in the well-known passage from Matthew, with an obvious firmness: "And I say also unto thee, that thou art Peter, and upon this rock I will build my church; and the gates of hell shall not prevail against it." Still, this is the only passage throughout the four Gospels where the word "church" is used. Today, in a world of many bureaucracies, in a world of two billion people, organized in all sorts of ways, the word *church* has quite a different connotation than the same word had centuries ago in the wilderness of Judaea. When He used the Aramaic word for *church* (*quahela*, or *kenishta*) He had in mind a group of people who were loyally committed to His teachings, and through Him and what He said, to God Almighty. Nor did He, of course, spell out precisely what Peter was to do. Indeed, a bit further in the Gospel of Matthew we are told that Jesus had this to say: "For where two or three are gathered together in my name, there am I in the midst of them."

For centuries biblical exegetes have argued over the significance of the passages I have just quoted from Matthew—and when reading them, as with the reading of the entire Bible, a reader's faith will tell him or her what to believe. I bring up these sections from the New Testament because they have a great bearing on the southern religion Flannery O'Connor knew about, not to mention her own strong religious beliefs. For her, obviously, Christ's statement to Peter marks the beginning of the Roman Catholic Church—a moment in Christianity that became, over the centuries, a moment in a particular religious institution's life. For the evangelists I have met all over the South, and for their passionate listeners, the statement to the disciples by Christ was an important moment of sanction for all those who, over the generations, have met to be with Him, to beseech Him, very much on their own, so to speak—outside of all "principalities and powers," including the various available churches.

Such a possible disagreement of biblical interpretation had its historical parallel in the side-by-side development, for the first three or four centuries, of a Christianity that gradually crystallized into the Catholic Church and, as well, a Christianity that was essentially Gnostic in nature. By the latter one means a mystical faith, proclaimed in sects and groups scattered over space and time—a faith that emphasizes revelation, prophetic instruction, and healing, all connected to or transmitted by acts of initiation and consecration. The Christian Gnostics made a sharp distinction, as did their non-Christian forbears, between the worlds of good and evil, between the higher or spiritual world and the lower or material world. They equated the flesh with evil, with driving energies that crave expression or fulfillment at all costs. Freud's early descriptions of the id come across as right out of a second-century Gnostic portrayal of the Devil who resides in our bodies. On the other hand, there is the soul, and its distinct spiritual possibilities. Life was viewed as a constant engagement with our darker side, and potentially as a journey through various "worlds" and "spheres" toward a heaven of light, purity, good; in the Christian version, God and His son, Jesus Christ.

The Gnostics were strong on salvation as something fought for, as something hard sought, as something one needs divine help in obtaining—mediated, of course, through preachers, teachers, fellow voyagers on a pilgrimage. Christ was, needless to say, a historical redeemer; before Him, Gnostic sects, nevertheless, were not strangers to the notion of salvation. A specific person as the embodiment of that goal (*Σωτήρ*) was the Christian addition to a long-standing preoccupation, among some Gnostics, with a way out of this earthly (devilish) existence. And the Christian Gnostics were as stubbornly ascetic, contemptuous of and afraid of the flesh as their predecessors in the pagan world. The Christian Gnostics embraced Paul, especially; hugged him too hard, it might be said—thereby distorting his overall message. He became for them a means of severely condemning the flesh, which was seen as worthless, the repository of everything dark and vicious —with no saving, balancing virtues.

Some of the Gnostics took Paul's welcome to the Gentiles, and attacks upon the Pharisees, as an excuse for a rather severe effort at dissociation from the Old Testament, whose moments of sensuality, and essential accommodation to the material were considered anathema.

In its extreme, but not rare, forms early Christian Gnosticism became a *raison d'etre* for an intensely ascetic, monastic life: no sex, and a denial of the body that became punitively lacerating. In its more moderate manifestations, this early Christian Gnosticism took the form of scattered groupings of emotionally excited, passionately spiritual people who placed themselves in the most immediate, direct, and continuing relationship with the Divine One, Christ, and who in search of Him depended upon the guidance of charismatic leaders. These individuals resorted to a mix of exhortation, storytelling, symbolic gesture, prognostication, denunciation, and strong insistence upon scrupulous self-scrutiny—all in the interests of a movement toward the higher realm, a release from this bondage to the netherworld of biological appetites. The leaders and teachers were, really, storytellers; they came up with imaginative constructions, with ideas of what was and will be, with mythological recitals, with dire pronouncements, with glowing promises—in the context, again, of a deteriorating political and cultural world.

Moreover, those tight-knit Gnostic sects, however Christian by avowal of loyalty to Jesus Christ as Savior, became an ironic rallying ground for other, antagonistic elements in early Christianity—elements which would, in time, coalesce into an institution, a structure of authority and tradition, the Roman Catholic Church. The "practical heresies" Flannery O'Connor observed and responded to, as a writer, were the very same ones her Church has taken critical notice of, century after century. It can be argued, even, that her Church wouldn't be what it is, were not the Gnostics a constant presence; and were they not to crop up, again and again, throughout the long history of Christianity —not least, one twentieth-century American Catholic would say, in our southern states.

While the various Gnostic sects became Christian, there was a growing tendency in the first centuries toward a consolidation of *the* Church, whose religious sovereignty, jurisdiction, and prerogatives became issues strenuously contested. The Gnostics favored their kind of Diaspora: a highly personal and localist response to the Savior and the promise He was believed to offer; a release from the craven demands of the flesh; a spiritual flight to His heavenly kingdom. (Some of those same Gnostic sects occasionally fell prey to libertine excesses, lapses of faith and control as excessive and unrestrained as the ascetism was harsh and pitiless.) But those who were not Gnostics had quite another version of Christianity in mind; they wanted order—amidst seeming chaos. They sought visible signs of order, of discipline, of regulation—of continuity in command, of reliability of presence, of certainty of doctrine. They welcomed the development of a hierarchy. They greeted with enthusiasm an explicit and authorized canon of the Holy Scriptures. They wanted not just individual confessions of faith, but *rules* of faith—notions shared with others about what ought to be believed and practiced, what is out of bounds.

Very important, those building the foundation of the Roman Catholic Church feared the dualism of Gnosticism—its insistence that the mind and soul be freed from the body. A number of intellectuals, naturally, were attracted to Gnosticism; its pre-Christian roots went back to Plato—the effort to connect the intellectual and the moral life. But the "Gnosis" of knowledge became, ultimately, the "Gnosis" of mystical revelation. The early Church was lucky to be spared a struggle with a band of self-important intellectuals whose heady, abstract ideas asserted themselves with regard to the concrete, particular lives of a lesser breed: the ordinary human beings expected to swallow what was fed them. But the Gnostics did threaten an unstable era with the primacy of a quite fantastic mythology, only partially Christian in nature (devils of all sorts), as well as, again, a radical, excessive dualism (matter as against spirit), and in some instances, a dangerously intense antinomianism, with its high and mighty claim that no one's moral law meant all that much, once one devotes oneself to the Gospels, to a plea that Christ intercede for the soul. That last inclination was justified by a reading of Matthew (18:19): "Again I say unto you, That if two of you shall agree on earth as touching anything that they shall ask, it shall be done for them of my Father which is in heaven."

If one reads St. Augustine, one finds Gnosticism struggling for assertion, but fought off long and hard: the birlliant soul-searching of a mind in danger of giving evil far more sway than the Church was prepared to allow. Christ became incarnate; God had no evident horror of the flesh, per se. Augustine's effort for an honorable accommodation to his own self (to be at home in his flesh) is a recapitulation, brilliantly rendered in a psychologically subtle autobiography, of a widespread religious struggle in the early Christian Church—a struggle by no means concluded, even today. Augustine battled Manichaeism, which became, really, a new kind of Gnosticism in the fourth and fifth centuries; and whites or blacks of Baldwin County, Georgia, do likewise as they assemble (some of them) out of the sight of main-street churches, and, often enough, grant unto Satan powers others would reserve for God and Christ. Augustine tried to balance faith with authority, emotion with reason, the capacity in us for good with the inclination we have to transgress God's laws, an inclination which he knew, finally, must not be itself deified. His struggle was later carried on within the Catholic Church under different names: the Albigensian heretics, who saw the Church as itself possessed by the Devil—corrupt, not by individualism, but by reflection of an enormous struggle between Heaven and Hell, Light and Darkness, Satan and God; and the Marcionite heretics, inspired by Marcion, one of the so-called Docetae, who denied the physical reality of Christ, and dismissed all matter as hopelessly corrupt—a way of emphasizing the distinction between apparent (δοκέιν, to appear) and the real; and later on, the Jansenists, who, in the seventeenth century, took up the cudgels, yet again, for total depravity as a correct approximation of man's nature.

All of that abstract doctrinal history can be overheard, can be seen, Miss O'Connor knew. Her own theological sophistication enabled her to connect the sights and sounds of back-country, southern twentieth-century life to a history that began in Christ's time, and even before. She was a novelist, but she was also enough of a church historian to be able to summon one of those "frames of reference" a number of us social scientists find it desirable to impose upon the seeming flux of things. The ascetism and antisacerdotal preaching of the twelfth- and thirteenth-century Catharist heretics (so-called Albigenses) were understood rather well by one Milledgeville resident of our century.

Who is Hazel Motes, the central figure in *Wise Blood*? As with all of Miss O'Connor's writing, an enormous amount of attention has been devoted to the religious symbolism in the novel, to the point that, again, one hesitates to add another word. Yet, in her letters, only published in 1979, she makes clear just how intricately theological her mind was, as it set to work embodying philosophical knowledge, and no small amount of church history, in a series of stories. In the author's note that she provided the second edition of *Wise Blood*, published two years before her death, she gives a brief hint of her intentions: Hazel Motes is a "Christian *malgre lui*." She directly challenges her admiring readers by pointing out that, whereas they might admire the character Hazel for trying to rid himself of certain (Christian) obsessions, she admires him for not being able to do so. She admires him for the impediments he did not overcome—spiritual, not psychological, in nature. She admires him, it can be argued, for the struggle he waged, in the Augustinian tradition, against the Manichaeism which has always threatened the Catholic Church.

Her principal figure in the novel is the grandson of a Tennessee backwoods preacher. Hazel's mother is also a fundamentalist Christian, fighting sin at every turn. Hazel knew "by the time he was twelve years old that he was going to be a preacher." And he knew, from his childhood on, "a deep black wordless conviction," that if he was going to avoid the kind of hounding, ever watchful and scourging Jesus his grandfather evoked, there was only one way possible: "to avoid sin." Wasn't he, to the grandfather's mind, "a mean sinful unthinking boy," whom, nevertheless, Jesus would chase "over the waters of sin" to have! The grandfather, who screamed sin and Jesus—polarities—had no church; he preached "on the nose" of his "Ford automobile." The grandfather had "a preacher's power," located by his creator, ever so shrewdly, in the man's "neck and tongue and arm." The brain and heart are not so necessary. The people of Eastrod, we are told, had little hope; they were going straight to Hell, the grandfather knew—but for the personal, charismatic effect he had on them, as an agent of Christ's "soul-hungry" interest in everyone.

Now, with one additional letter, Eastrod becomes Eastroad—an Eastern Cross. The Gnostics, the various Manichaean prophets of early Christianity, flourished in the eastern part of the Roman Empire. It was an Oriental dualism that gave Christian Gnosticism much of its ideological thrust; and needless to say, the decadent antiquity of the first centuries after Christ was quite ready for such a penetration. Evil seemed ready to grasp the world; one could only hope and pray that the balance might one day be redressed. Those who deferred to Satan made sense to those who found themselves in a crumbling social and political situation: Barbarian hordes from without, and an impossibly corrupt civil authority from within. Out of such a Gnostic inheritance comes Hazel Motes—his eyes, at birth, hazy and with motes or dust obscuring his vision. This blindness is transmitted from generation to generation—heresies that don't vanish, as the Church well knows; but, as the author insists, heresies that are preferable by far to what obtains in Taulkinham, where Hazel is headed: the New South, the South of pornography and moviehouses and commerce and a vast indifference to anything religious.

The signs Hazel sees as he approaches this southern city tell us of *its* preoccupations—not with sin and darkness and the weakness of the flesh, but "Peanuts," "Western Union," "Ajax," "Taxi," "Hotel," "Candy." These signs are impersonal ("electric") rather than handwritten, yet they "blinked frantically." The author is comparing visions of the world: Eastrod's as against Taulkinham's, Hazel Motes's, as against those of the assorted would-be followers and leaders he meets. He is come to preach the "church of truth without Jesus Christ Crucified." He is dressed in a preacher's dark suit and black hat, and he shows obvious charismatic gifts. Is he the anti-Christ—the Satan many of the Gnostics conjured up as a force not necessarily second to that of God's? If Motes is that ultimate Devil, or an agent thereof, he has scruples which, interestingly enough (the author's searing critique of modern civilization?), make *our* various contemporary devils much more conniving and cynical than anything, say, the colleagues of St. Augustine, caught up in Manichaeism, ever dreamed possible.

One Hoover Shoats wants to turn Motes's ministry into something quite profitable—offer people what they want. When Motes says no, someone else is found who says yes. What is his name? Solace Layfield—an uncompromising jab at the South's, at America's Taulkinhams and what their residents want out of religion: a bit of reassurance, maybe some sex therapy in the parish hall, as part of an "encounter group approach" to what might well, these days, be called "the problems of making it: sex and religion in the modern world." Shoats strums his with-it guitar, calls people "friends," not "sinners," and tells them that he wants to "innerduce" them "to the True Prophet here and I want you all to listen to his words because I think they're going to make you happy like they've made me!" Hazel's rage at Solace Layfield is, however, quite clearly a rage of self-recognition. He is driving the Essex, and is bent on denying Christ—sinning as boldly as possible: if God is dead, or nonexistent, why not?

The blind lead the blind; and the blind destroy the blind, the author reminds us: wars and revolutions, false prophets and corrupt principalities and powers everywhere. We are not allowed to turn Hazel into Good and Solace into Evil; rather, we are reminded that there is something in Hazel that may save him, that may make him, at some future time, different from what he seems to be—another doomed heretic. He kills another heretic; he rids himself of sinners he happens to detest (the more so because they remind him of himself). He indulges himself in what others call sin, thereby defying them, provoking in the world (he vainly hopes) a call to arms such as he advocates. Yet, something in him won't let the matter rest there. He is not only a flagrant sensualist, a cynical murderer. He is on a journey—a pilgrim determined to preach, to take on the world forcefully. His path is littered with seductive temptations, obstacles and threats of various kinds. He might become a religious phony. No, he won't. He kills off that possibility. He might join company with Enoch Emery, the sad, lonely youth who desperately wants to follow Motes, do his every command, and not least be a heretical accomplice of his. No to that, also.

In a fascinating scene, we are by indirection given a lesson in the Oriental occultism that was, historically, such a significant part of the early Christian Gnosticism. Emery has all kinds of rituals, symbolic gestures, signs and symbols in his mind; he wants to share them with Motes, the beginning of a Gnostic sect. Every day he has his milkshake, carries on with a waitress, goes to the zoo and carries on with the animals, and then, moment by moment, truth by truth, finds his way to a nearby museum, in which a mummy resides—of no meaning to anyone but this would-be cultist and his would-be leader. Enoch not only shows this mummy triumphantly to Motes (who is bored, and well able to resist that particular temptation) but goes on to steal it, call it, even, "the new jesus." Hazel destroys it—a heretical posture refused. There are all sorts of rites, ceremonies, relics, signals, symbols that Motes finds available as he walks his way through this life; he is a southern preacher-pilgrim coming to terms with invitations, seductions, corruptions. For example: Asa Hawks, who simulates blindness. He is a representation of the diabolic, satanic lower world. He is a liar; his daughter a fickle, amoral companion in Evil.

We wonder, as this fellow Motes works his way through scene after scene, what the author intends. Some critics have called the episode with Enoch Emery distracting and of no real consequence—an interlude worked into the novel's progression, which is meant to characterize a believer's search. But if the reader takes all that Motes experiences as symbolically instructive (though wonderfully concrete), then the question has to be: symbolic of what? A single thematic element that accounts for virtually everything in the novel is that of heresy: a determined Christian's pitfalls. Heretics, the author wants to make clear, are not thieves and liars; they are, inevitably, part of Taulkinham's (the South's, America's) population. An Enoch Emery tells us what a desperately hurt, vulnerable, abandoned, marginal people can turn to—an effort to make sense of their situation. Miss O'Connor meant what she said: "practical heresies." She did not set herself up as a judge, or a Vatican theologian. Her affection for Enoch is obvious; he receives from her the seriousness of comic inspection. What has he to fall back on, to believe—this forlorn youth? Who in Taulkinham cares about him at all? Scorned by others, rejected and cut off, shut off, he tries to find an answer for himself to the bad riddle of his apparently negligible life. Somehow he will distinguish himself, make the world, if not eternity, pay attention. And he does: wearing a monkey suit, he can make a mark for himself.

The other animals in the jungle that is Taulkinham have no such candor, no such awareness of what, if anything, they want out of life —beyond the state of being "happy," mentioned by Hoover Shoats. In a brilliant polemic against rootless twentieth-century urban life (an attack the Agrarians would have appreciated), and additionally, on its sustaining modern heresies of logical positivism and materialism, Miss O'Connor has Motes deliver the following sermon: "I preach there are all kinds of truth, your truth and somebody else's truth," he called. "No truth behind all truths is what I and this church preach! Where you come from is gone, where you thought you were going to never was there, and where you are is no good unless you can get away from it. Where is there a place for you to be? No place." And a bit further: "In yourself right now is all the place you've got." So much for Gauguin and his great Tahiti testimonial painting (1897), with its questions: *D'oú venons nous? Que sommes nous? Oú allons nous?* So much for anyone who has ever asked those existentialist questions. We are left with ourselves, our contemporary self-centeredness, our various narcissistic cults: the body, the mind, health, sex, exercise, food—the best-seller list with its "revelations" about what we consider important, if not our version of a "revelation."

In the end Hazel Motes turns away from Taulkinham. He knows what Thomas Wolfe needed a longer time, traveled farther, and took more pages to discover—that there is no return to the shared, everyday "practical heresies" of Eastrod, where an impoverished, uneducated southern population finds through a mixture of self-accusation and messianic, ceremonial contractual agreement a kind of release from the never-ending frustrations and harsh obligations of the rural lowlife. Nor does Taulkinham's "progress" offer anything better—as the author in her choice of names for, say, Atlanta more than implies: talk, talk, talk. Hustlers. Pornographers. Crooks. Liars. Of all ages. Of both sexes. Flannery O'Connor is called by many critics a conservative; she was criticized for not taking after, publicly, the segregationist South. What she wanted to conserve, good Catholic that she was, might be called the Church's authority, its truth—nowhere in evidence among the lost souls of a hellish Taulkinham. What she wanted to condemn, through resort to bitter humor, magnificently painted symbols, suggestive ironies, all worked into an unfolding narrative, was not any particular vanity, or piece of pagan idolatry (white skin) but the much larger canvas, of which the South had become, she knew, all too much a part: a decadent modernity with its very own way of living out various heresies—more than a match for the maneuvers adopted by a decadent antiquity.

In the end, Hazel Motes blinds himself, puzzles and frustrates the landlady, Mrs. Flood, who cares for him, and begins (in another sense of the expression) to care for him, but who can only go so far toward him, or certainly, along with him on the journey he is making. It is glib to pass Motes off as a "Christ-figure," a cliché of literary criticism —and an ironic one, indeed: Christ as someone who helps writers mold their characters. Motes came to a city full of clever, glib people, and one of them, Asa Hawks, pretends to be blind: the prophet who supposedly has lacerated his body in proof of his faith. Motes ends up forsaking his ministry, and various temptations, to follow in the Asa Hawks tradition. He does blind himself—but not as part of a confidence game; nor in any effort to form a heretical sect. This is no rural preacher handling snakes, browbeating people, celebrating pain and suffering as virtues. This is a man who has renounced rites and rituals, promises and threats. He is no "Christ figure"; he is no representative of Satan, either. He is one of us, a suffering human being, blind as the rest of us, but someone who at least knows it. He is a vulnerable human being; like the rest of us he will die. He has given up an interest in persuading others of anything; he no longer has any ideas about who should believe what.

His remaining time on earth is characterized by self-laceration, resignation, an inscrutable indifference to the conventional, the "normal." The barbed wire, "wrapped around his chest," makes him a penitent of sorts—but in the tradition of monkhood rather than evangelism. This is, to draw upon David Riesman's manner of description, an "inner-directed" kind of ascetism, rather than the "outer-directed" kind of preaching an earlier Motes practiced. A personal struggle with heresy, rather than a programmatic moral broadcast. A man saying goodbye to this earth, rather than one set upon persuading it along lines congenial to his beliefs—or his personal (these days called "emotional") requirements. A man looking inward (the meaning of blindness in this case?) rather than abroad the land—and inward in preparation for the longest possible expedition. A man called, rather than giving vent to his own wishes—*his* calling. Called by whom? Separated by whom from the increasingly touching affections of his landlady? She obviously wants to be not only a conventional companion (his wife) but someone who caught a glimpse, to use a word that ironically seems to fit, of his vision, and would like a bit more: "Watching his face had become a habit with her; she wanted to penetrate the darkness behind it and see for herself what was there."

It is clear, by now, that a determined heretic has become a self-sacrificing monk of a kind—and as monks have often been, an object of curiosity, wonder, envy, resentment, ridicule. This is not a boasting, manipulative ascetic, prepared to use self-flagellation as an instrument of psychological and material self-gain. One sees a variety of asceticism in parts of the South (and elsewhere) as evidence of the persistence (inevitable, perhaps, given human nature) of Manichaeism; and one also sees ascetism in Appalachia and stretches of the Black Belt harnessed to entrepreneurial religiosity. Surely all monks have struggled with the former temptation; and some monks, even some orders, at points of time in the world's history, may have gone awry in the latter direction. But Miss O'Connor knows how especially vulnerable Protestant sectarianism, and specifically, the more anarchic, out-of-the-way demonstrations of Christian passion, can end up being, with respect to that quite exploitative (and for some, all too beckoning) commodity: suffering and its satisfactions, its excitements.

Hazel Motes's last words are, simply, "I want to go on where I'm going"—an inscrutable traveler telling no one of any direction, and rather, allowing the motions of grace, utterly mysterious, to carry him along. In contrast, there are others who know the propaganda value of a show of pain. "I'm hurting; I'm hurting for Jesus," we heard an evangelist boast to a north Georgia audience in 1963. Then followed an odd mélange of ideas, proposals, interpretations—evidence for anyone who needed it that Flannery O'Connor, among other things, was a southern realist, utterly in touch with a segment of the world around her:

> We're all hurting; but we won't admit it. Oh, sweet pain! Oh, delicious pain! When we're not in pain, we're cut off from God. Didn't Jesus meet his God on the Cross, the nails in Him! He didn't say hello to God, sitting in a big house, the air-conditioner on, and television going. He had nails in Him. I tell you, I remind you: nails. He meant for us to follow Him, and be like Him. He meant for us to suffer—and then there will be the Kingdom of Heaven! It's hard here; it's a tough life. God meant it to be that way. He didn't have a picnic here, so why should we!
>
> This integration business: what a waste of time and money. You won't get into Heaven by integrating your kids in a school. You won't get into Heaven by winning all the battles. If you lose, you win the biggest battle of them all. I was sick, and in the hospital, and they wanted to give me medicine, to kill the pain, and I said, no sir, doctor, and no ma'am, nurse: I'll lie in this bed and suffer, and consider myself a lucky man! I heard a colored woman on the television, and she said—I felt real bad for her!—that she was going to see a better life for her kids, through this integration, and there would be an end to the

suffering. *An end to the suffering*; when I heard her say that, I wanted to grab her, and tell her—say this to her: Mrs. Colored Woman, you're in real trouble! Oh, yes! Real bad trouble—oh, yes! If Jesus Christ Almighty didn't think He'd ever see "an end to the suffering," until He got back to Heaven, with God, then why should any of us have such an idea! I say, suffering is ours! I say, we should welcome suffering! It's a sign; we're told that God is challenging us!

I was making coffee the other morning, and the water spilled, and my arm got the hot water on it, and there was pain. For sure, there was pain. And you know something: I thought of God, and all *He* went through, a nail through His right hand and a nail through His left hand, and His feet nailed to the Cross as well, and I cried for Jesus, and I thought to myself: it's not much, it's not much at all, having your arm burned with a little water. Those who suffer most are going to see the Kingdom of Heaven; it's His promise. Those who have an easy life, are going to meet Mr. Satan, down there in Hell; that was the Lord's promise, too. So it's not integration that should be pushing us on; and it's not a lot of greed, to become top man on the ladder; it's Jesus Christ who should be on our minds, day and night, and if there's pain that comes to us, then Lord, be grateful, because He's showing you a sign that He cares for you. Of course, don't forget it: there may be other signs, and the day may come when God decides to shake everything up, like it says in the Bible, the only book that counts in the whole wide world.

In "Revelation," we're told that it all gets turned upside down, and you won't have the world like it is, anymore. And maybe a lot of those big, rich, city folks, and the federal government, and the ones who run the banks, and sell the stocks, and the integration people—they'll all be seen floating down some river, and it'll be taking them, dead as can be, to the gates of Hell, and won't that be a sight for sore eyes! And if you don't like what you're seeing, you just turn away from the sins, and you try to be a *Christian*, and nothing else, and don't you let anyone, no one in the government, and none of these ministers with their big fat salaries and their churches so large you can fit an army in them, and fancy brick and rugs from Asia and no good places like that—don't you let *anyone* point a finger and tell you what to believe, because it's between you and Jesus Christ and no one else, just like it was when He came down here and walked among us, and suffered: oh, did He!

Oh, was there more! Oh, did he go on—and on and on. Oh, did that handful of "good country people" go on and on and on; saying yes, and shouting for more, and more; clapping their hands and slapping their knees and staring up at the sky, and smiling with enormous enjoyment at each other and at the man with the mildly scalded arm. One or two looked at their own arms: unblemished. One or two glanced nervously at their own hands: no blood. One or two moved their feet at the mention of His feet. Who is anyone to speak for the intentions of others? But we felt, at the time, that if the evangelist had asked those fifty or so people to hurt themselves significantly, a number of them would have done so! Blind themselves? Maybe not. Flannery O'Connor did not live to read about the Reverend Jones and the fate of his Guyana flock. Had she written a story with such a scenario, she would have strained not only her readers' credulity, but her critics' patience: the grotesque indulged far too excessively. And no doubt southern evangelists deserve to be carefully distinguished from West Coast cultists. In the rural South there is a long tradition for the kind of antitraditional religious expression cited immediately above. Still, as one goes through such remarks, and edits them down to a fairly readable, pungent summary, one is struck by the theme of asceticism, by the embrace of Manichaean dualism, by the recommendation of pain as evidence of grace. One is struck, too, by the mix of populism, racism, conservatism, nationalism, anarchism.

Here was a preacher (one of many we've heard these past two decades) railing against all religious conventions, all institutions, save that of the informal assembly of his kindred souls: the tradition of Southern Evangelical Protestantism, if one is to be categorical. A tradition with its own, casual but real constraints. This preacher was an itinerant, a man with a car and the Book. He came, was given hospitality and left—his (white, rural) listeners nearer to God, and not incidentally, confirmed in many of their social, political, and economic views. The minister also was nearer to God, so he believed, and not incidentally, he had some "pocket cash," the phrase he used when he asked for something to "keep going with," as he moved on: another county, another evening "vigil before the eyes of God." As for the resort to ocular imagery, the suggestion that one not see what is sinful, the suggestion that God is watching us ever so carefully, it is no big step from all that to Hazel Motes, never mind Oedipus Rex. Flannery O'Connor knew the desperation of such people, knew their "unconscious pride," knew the "ridiculous religious predicaments" they got themselves into, knew the "practical heresies" they found for themselves—in an attempt to soften a hard fate, or maybe, like the Greek tragic figure, acknowledge the hand of that hard fate. And she knew, very important, the "grimly comic" side to all of that—a revival as a show, as a theater unworthy, perhaps, of Sophocles' genius, but in keeping with his wish to reach, to touch, to prompt amazement, fascination, surprise, and a strong release of emotion (catharsis).

Her story "Parker's Back" was, for us, at first reading, almost too much to be true—because it was full of so much lived, southern truth: the sociology of religion turned by magic into a funny and sad tale. Rather obviously, Parker's wife is in the grand Manichaean tradition: "She was plain, plain." And more to the point, "She was forever sniffing up sin." In a wonderful sentence the author gives us an entire scene she had plenty of reason to know about: "She did not smoke or dip, drink whiskey, use bad language or paint her face, and God knew some paint would have improved it, Parker thought." The "God knew" is a fine, leavening interpolation; and God knows what such a parenthetical expression can set going in parts of Miss O'Connor's home state, among others. Sometimes a quiet, grateful, tension-breaking laugh; sometimes a stern reproving glance—a look as if the saved had spotted in horror the damned. But early on we begin to wonder, as the author intends for us to, as Parker did, in his own way: why should he have married "this ugly woman?" This woman whose "terrible bristly claw slammed the side of his face" at the beginning of the story (he is overheard swearing); this woman who grabs a broom and beats and beats Parker's back at the end of the story, because the man all tatooed-up had gone and had a picture put on the one remaining expanse of flesh still available: "behaloed head of a flat stern Byzantine Christ with all-demanding eyes."

A deceptively slim plot holds together a powerful and wonderfully humorous foray, once more, into the South's backwoods religious life. Parker is in no way dismissed as a suffering fool—or as it might be thought, these days, a masochist whose problems have affected his interpersonal relationships! (In one of her blunt letters, Miss O'Connor might not have been able to resist a parenthetical comment of a single word after such tiresome, stupid language: horrors! Some of us might want to use a stronger word.) Parker is, in fact, a southern farm boy existentialist. When we learn that "his neck began to prickle," we remind ourselves how much Miss O'Connor favored Walker Percy's novel, *The Moviegoer*, whose soul-searching hero is continually expressing his bewilderment, his curiosity about the meaning of life, through such physical signs—not symptoms. At the age of fourteen Parker had known awe—"a man in a fair, and tatooed from head to foot." The man's grace: his muscles flexed "so that the arabesque of men and beasts and flowers on his skin appeared to have a subtle motion of its own." Right clever, the southern reader says to himself or herself—as with the peacock in "The Displaced Person": an intimation of divine glory rendered so concrete as to prompt an ironic secondary awe, this time in the person holding a book, reading a story. And the comparison: "Parker was filled with emotion, lifted up as some people are when the flag passes." Those "some people" are Parker's people, are Flannery O'Connor's people, are southerners who still have no intention (say what "they" will, up there, "in those places," as we've heard the North collectively called) of turning their backs, so to speak, on the United States of America, *and* its flag, *and* its national anthem, *and* the prayers that get spoken in classrooms, not the least significant part of which is the commendation to God Almighty that He take it upon Himself constantly and with special consideration to bless and watch over this American land.

Pointedly, the author tells us that "until he saw the man at the fair, it did not enter his [Parker's] head that there was anything out of the ordinary about the fact that he existed." And when his head did start realizing the (existentialist) situation he was in, as a human being, the awareness took a form all too familiar to those who have read Sartre and Camus, and once more, Walker Percy: "A peculiar unease settled in him." Right after that notation, we have a simile that connects a story with a novel, an early writing effort with a much later one: "It was as if a blind boy had been turned so gently in a different direction that he did not know his destination had been changed." Blindness, the author knows, can be a religious condition as well as an ophthalmological one. Who of us can really see where we come from and where we're headed to? "Are we not all blind, wandering in the desert, waiting for a voice to direct us, a hand to come touch us?" That last question was asked by the evangelist quoted above. Hazel Motes and the young Parker: two blind but searching southern "boys."

As with Hazel, our young Parker came from a religious "background," all right. And from a certain quite specifically indicated class "background." He attended a "trade school." He worked in a garage. His mother worked in a laundry. He was a beer drinker. As a youth he fought a lot with other kids. He wanted more and more tatoos on his adolescent body; they helped him with girls. Meanwhile, his mother "wept over what was becoming of him." She took him to a revival. He didn't know where he was going until "he saw the big lighted church." He bolted. The next day he fled to the navy; he wandered the world, collecting more and more of his beloved skin pictures: a tiger, a panther, a cobra, hawks, the queen of England (Elizabeth II) and her husband, Philip, "a few obscenities." Five years later he was discharged, dishonorably: drinking, a leave without permission—what someone "poor" and "uneducated" and with a history of "trouble" often does in the military. Parker returns to his roots: he "decided that country air was the only kind fit to breathe." The author condenses commerce and theology in a single sentence as she tells us what he did with himself: "At the time he met his future wife, he was buying apples by the bushel and selling them for the same price by the pound to isolated homesteaders on back country roads." Doing so, he heard himself (or, rather, his tattoos) appraised as "vanity of vanities." It is his future wife speaking. She eventually eats one of his apples; she takes it "quickly," chews on it "slowly." This Eve of the Southland's small village life turns out to be the daughter of "a Straight Gospel preacher," who is described as "away, spreading it in Florida." A wonderful verb, that last one. And a wonderfully revealing place turns out to be the scene of the Parker marriage: the County Ordinary's office—"because Sarah Ruth thought churches were idolatrous."

Soon the preacher's child is pregnant. We are told a second time that she is "ugly"; and we notice more bodily signs being dispatched by her husband, "a little tic in the side of his face," this time a reflection of irritability. We learn that Parker is twenty-eight; like Binx Bolling in *The Moviegoer,* he is about to enter "the middle way" (T. S. Eliot). And, baling hay, with an old woman's "sorry" machine, he experiences the beginning of a conversion. This Saul turns to Paul as he rides, stares at the sun, suddenly sees a tree reaching out for him, feels himself yanked into the air. "GOD ABOVE!" is what he yells. He lands "on his back" (soon to be tattooed) and the tractor crashes into the tree, goes up in flames—the second time Miss O'Connor has a machine precipitating an intense spiritual crisis in one of those Georgia pasturelands. Parker joins Mrs. McIntyre of "The Displaced Person": a "great change in his life" has taken place. Whereas she is much older, and can only think back and wonder what might have been, he is about to take "a leap forward." He knows in his bones that he awaits a painful future ("a worse unknown") but he is helpless, he also knows, before something mysteriously compelling. (The Flannery O'Connor reader knows to guess, at this point, that divine grace, in all its terrible power, is at work.)

He is after a tattoo; he is after God. When the tattoo is being applied on his back, by an artist he finds, Parker is especially interested in the eyes. Parker wanted God's notice, and only His. As the artist works along, Parker gets a preliminary look, through the manipulation of mirrors, at what is being done. The authorial voice describes what he saw this way: "It was almost completely covered with little red and blue and ivory and saffron squares; from them he made out the lineaments of the face—a mouth, the beginning of heavy brows, a straight nose, but the face was empty; the eyes had not been put in. The impression for the moment was almost as if the artist had tricked him and done the Physician's Friend." Parker's wife was evidently the captive of one version of the Gnostic heresy—an extreme devaluation of the body in favor of asceticism—but Parker was not himself going to succumb to another version of Gnosticism, the kind the author of "Parker's Back" knew all too well: the excessive emphasis on mind, on ideas, that "liberal humanists" are quite comfortable with. If there is nothing inherently spiritual about suffering, per se, then there is also nothing inherently spiritual about nice, friendly thoughts directed at one's neighbors. Or so one writer believed, and with her, in his own way, the outraged Parker, who wasn't out to have his back become a resting place for some sweet contemporary piety.

As the artist completes his work on the tattoo, he converses with Parker. The substance of their brief exchange tells us a lot about the difference between Southern Evangelical Protestantism and Miss O'Connor's Catholicism; it is her genius to have asserted that distinction through the apparently innocent, unpretentious, matter-of-fact conversation of two southern country fellows. The tattoo artist asks Parker, "Have you gone and got religion? Are you saved?" The reply is a brief "Naw," followed by, "I ain't got no use for none of that. A man can't save hisself from whatever it is he don't deserve none of my sympathy." It is his wife who considers herself saved, he goes on to emphasize. To save oneself is an individual's task, and one can't declare oneself "saved"—or get saved by ritualistic denial of this or that or even just about everything. One's soul requires the exertion of intelligent, discriminating action; one's soul is connected to one's freedom: we are put here with the God-given permission of a Creator to fend for ourselves, spiritually. That is the divine charge; not a faith of Calvinist determinism, nor one of tricky manipulations through which the damned do things they're told to do, then in turn get told that they're "saved."

With the tattoo on him, Parker is full of turmoil. He downs a pint of whiskey fast, gets into a poolroom brawl, ends up in an alley, "examining his soul." The result? We are told that "he saw [his soul] as a spider web of facts and lies." Yet, he saw something else, too: "The eyes that were now forever on his back were eyes to be obeyed." And on the way home: "It was as if he were himself but a stranger to himself, driving into a new country though everything he saw was familiar to him, even at night." Once home, he wants to offer what we begin to realize is a certain grace, the reward of a personal search, to his wife. He knocks on her door, makes himself known, against her considerable resistance: the deaf ears of the idolatrous. We are told that "his spider web soul" has turned into "a perfect arabesque of colors, a garden of trees and birds and beasts." But not for Sarah Ruth, who, seeing her husband's back, can only scream "Idolatry!" tell him that God is "a spirit," remind him that "no man shall see his [God's] face," proceed to go after him, beating "large welts" on nothing less than "the face of the tattooed Christ."

This is a subtle but strong assault on what was for the author a fierce kind of paganism. Motes's heresy is undone in the course of his own life; we are quite connected to him, in sympathy with him, by the end—though, of course, his real conversation, by the last pages, is with God, not his landlady, hence her talkativeness and his relative silence. But Sarah Ruth's heresy is there, unyielding—a given fact of the southern landscape. There is nothing in her appearance, her manner or her language that comes across as in the least inviting. As for Parker, his Christian "existentialist" search is quite apparent. In this late story of

O'Connor's, published some months after her death, one sees very much at work her philosophical knowledge: the Gabriel Marcel she read, the Walker Percy essays, as well as his first novel, she also read. Parker as a drinking, fighting, wandering sensualist (Kierkegaard's "aesthetic stage"). Parker as a reflecting person who is trying to figure out why—and what to do (Kierkegaard's "ethical stage"). And finally, Parker who seems, at times, strangely resigned to his fate—someone in touch with God, to Whom he seems mystically called. (A suggestion of Kierkegaard's "resignation"—the full-fledged surrender to God's will.)

The foregoing is all too abstract, however. One can assume with Flannery O'Connor an extremely sophisticated theological mind at work. Her correspondence lays to rest any question about that! But she was not writing an essay on religion. Her relatively short, short story, "Parker's Back," combines a fluidity of narration, an adroit shaping of character, the effective and suggestive use of dialect, in the service of an unfolding drama. The author tucked in her Christian existentialism, her *Catholic* existentialism, without burdening the story, or distracting the reader, who is all caught up in his or her involvement with these unfortunate, sad, very funny, rather wily people, and the southern landscape, of which they at times seem mere appendages.

Flannery O'Connor knew how perverse a certain kind of revivalism can become. The New Testament is used as a whip. The Incarnation is thrown aside; "the word become flesh" gets turned into anathema. The Old Testament is either shunned altogether, as one witnesses among those members of the Klan (or its sympathizers) who are also determined "believers," or the moral sternness of Jeremiah and Isaiah and Amos and Ezekiel receive a single-minded attention—as if the Psalms, for instance, were never written, spoken, handed down over the generations. All of that has to do with the Marcionite heresy—a stripping of God not only from His flesh, so to speak, but His heritage, His roots (as it is put these days), His stated ancestral tradition. "This is Jesus, the King of the Jews," the "accusation" said—over His head as He hung from the cross. But a definition was also thereby being asserted: a particular man, who belonged to a particular people, who lived (among many others) in a particular empire, and at a particular time in the empire's lifespan: God's chosen entrance into history.

With such knowledge firmly in her mind, she observed once that "the Hebrew genius for making the absolute concrete has conditioned the southerner's way of looking at things." In his translations from the Bible and his writing on it as a narrative, Reynolds Price, another southerner, has echoed her sentiments. *A Palpable God*, the title he gave, tells what novelists such as he and O'Connor have great skill in doing—dealing with the Divinity through storytelling. She knew that many of her fellow Catholics, especially those who lived outside the South, were somewhat estranged from the Bible. She observed once that it "has not penetrated very far into our consciousness nor conditioned our reactions to experience." She pointed out that "unfortunately, where you find Catholics reading the Bible, you find that it is usually a pursuit of the educated." The Church's rituals and liturgy have their distinct life—connected to the Bible, of course, but also possessed of their own authority. In the Evangelical Protestantism of the South, the Bible, in all its complexity, holds undisputed sway. Miss O'Connor reminds her readers that "in the South the Bible is known by the ignorant as well [as the educated], and is always that *mythos* which the poor hold in common that is most valuable to the fiction writer." And the writer in her continues: "When the poor hold sacred history in common, they have ties to the Universal and the holy, which allows the meaning of their every action to be heightened and seen under the aspect of eternity." And further on, in a more autobiographical vein: "When you write about backwoods prophets, it is very difficult to get across to the modern reader that you take these people seriously, that you are not making fun of them, but that their concerns are your own and, in your judgment, central to human life."

She knew, and admitted that those so-called "backwoods prophets" and their avid listeners were for her "antidotes" of a kind. There is, she pointed out, an "overemphasis on the legal and logical" in the Church's attitude toward the believer and his or her faith—all too many categories, rules, regulations, prescriptions and proscriptions. In the revivalist fires whose heat and light she drew upon for her writing, there is none of the arid legalism she mentioned as a hazard of Catholic religious life these days. She was not inclined to be sparing of Catholicism—or rather, some of its cultural expressions: "Of course this vapid Catholicism can't influence you except to want to be shut of it," she told one of her (Catholic) correspondents. She went further: "The Catholic influence has to come at a deeper level. I was brought up in the novena-rosary tradition too, but you have to save yourself from it someday or dry up." And, even more caustically, she refers to "a nice vapid-Catholic distrust of finding God in action of any range and depth.

She was more than implying that the conventional worship of a powerful, international Church has tamed the religious passion of its faithful; there is no room for the kind of personal drama one witnesses in the outdoor revivalism of, say, Baldwin County, during a warm spring evening, when the preacher is urging each person to "let the spirit out," and "talk to God, tell Him what you're thinking and what you're doing, and make Him part of your life." To do that, to work God into one's everyday life, with dignity and growing faith and a sensitive, strong piety, rather than the "vapid" kind—that is not easily any American's twentieth-century fate. Even in the outer precincts of the South, Miss O'Connor was right to notice that the possibilities for such a life-adventure are diminishing. To her friend William Sessions she commented, in 1960, "The traditional Protestant bodies of the South are evaporating into secularism and respectability and are being replaced on the grass roots level by all sorts of strange sects that bear not much resemblance to traditional Protestantism—Jehovah's Witnesses, snake-handlers, Free Thinking Christians, Independent Prophets, the swindlers, the mad, and sometimes the genuinely inspired.

It was from some of those souls, Georgia neighbors of hers, that she drew ideas, plots, notions of what to set her mind chewing on. "The true prophet is inspired by the Holy Ghost," she once declared, "not necessarily by the dominant religion of his region." She was, in that regard, struggling with a dualism of her own—as do the fervid, original-minded, wonderfully sly and boldly theatrical preachers, if not prophets, one hears in a South still not yet gone "Yankee-secular," as one Atlanta theologian sadly and apologetically described himself and his religious direction to us in 1961. The Holy Ghost, untethered to God and Jesus Christ, is an influence that can be called upon in strange moments, indeed and for strange purposes, unquestionably. If the Catholic Church can become a means for bargaining through gestures with Divinity, some of the revivalist churches in rural Georgia and other southern states can become places where the Holy Ghost, or Holy Spirit, gives sanction to devilishly entrepreneurial "believers."

Here is a woman from rural Georgia, a woman I came to know in the 1960s, a woman not unlike Mrs. Shortley in appearance, background, and faith speaking about her "time" with "a wonderful preacher"—who, alas, "turned," much to her dismay:

> He seemed to be the best Christian you could want. He prayed all the time. He told us he woke up, jumped out of bed, made sure his knees hit the floor, almost the same time as his feet. He read from the Bible, thinking the Lord might want to listen. He prayed to the Lord: a good day; a good, good day; please dear Lord, a good day. He went and visited people. He'd come knocking on our door, and he'd want to sit and talk, and he'd tell me about Jesus healing the sick, and healing the lame, and healing the people who had gone and lost their heads, and they weren't thinking right. He told us about Jesus in the temple. Jesus didn't trust a lot of those big folks, and they were leading all the Jews down the path to ruin. He went in and He tore the temple up—where they worshipped. I tell you, I'd like to tear up a few churches around here—all those big shot types who own them.
>
> The preacher would come and I'd listen, and then I couldn't think of going back to my work. I'd tell the children to hush. I'd tell the children that this was a man of Jesus, who came here, speaking God's words to us. My oldest boy would get sassy; he'd say that anyone can say he speaks for Jesus, but where's the proof! Fourteen years, he is! Fresh, oh is he fresh! But now I know it; he's a smart one. He has his eyes, and he can listen real good. He saw the bills in the man's coat pocket: twenty dollar bills! He told me. I told him he was going to burn in Hell, the way he was talking! But my son said he'd heard that the preacher was a devil of a man, and if we didn't tell him to stop coming here, and taking our money, we'd be the ones to burn in Hell, all of us!
>
> I didn't believe my son. That's where I went wrong. My husband uses the bottle after he comes in from the crops. That preacher got to me. He made me believe him. He turned me; he turned me around. I was seeing black where it was white, and white where it was black, if you know what I mean. I was going along with him. I was swallowing every word he sent in my direction. Pretty soon I wasn't standing and listening to him, and I wasn't sitting down and listening to him; but I was listening to him! And then one day, my husband got to see us. And I'll tell you, there's good justice hereabouts: the sheriff and the judge said my husband was right before God, and he was only trying to save me, his wife, and that was self-defense for him, and I was a victim, so what could I do! You see, there's God Almighty, and there's Satan, and I swear it can be hard to know between the two, sometimes, because the Scripture tells

us that the Lord was wonderful and smart and He knew how to do anything He wanted, and He could beat the doctors, and beat the priests of the temple, and beat the kings and emperors, if He wanted to. But we're told that the Devil is a smart one, too; and he can pull all of the tricks you can imagine, and then some. If you ask me: it's very few on this earth who can tell the difference between Jesus Christ and the Devil. People can turn on you. That preacher turned on me, I believe.

Maybe the poor preacher got all confused. That's what he told my husband, that the Devil can confuse us, and I think if my husband had just been willing to wait and listen for five minutes, the preacher would have walked out, and there'd have been no trouble. As it was, my husband had his hand on the trigger, and when the preacher told us he was sent by God to save us, and he was "a part of God," that's what he said, I got down on my knees, and then my husband pulled the trigger once, then a second time, and then he shot three bullets near me, two right in front and one behind, and I said: "I'm dead, I'm dead." And he was without mercy; he said to me I *should* be, and he walked out. And the next thing I knew, he was out there working, as if not a thing had happened. I just stayed on the floor, praying as hard as I could. When my son came in, he said he told me so. He threw me some clothes, and told me I'd better get ready to go to the county jail. But God didn't want me in jail, I guess. Oh, I hope and pray there's some answer to all this: why we're put here. It's a strange gift of God's, this life; but He walks away from us sometimes, and we're in trouble. Maybe He doesn't have the time for all of us. The Holy Spirit can desert you. That preacher told me the Holy Spirit was smiling on us. But I realize now that he made that smile up in his head. The Devil seized him. I always have wondered how anyone, even God Himself, can pay mind to all the people in this county, and then the others, in other counties, and all over Georgia. It's a mystery.

She had never heard of Flannery O'Connor, but she knew to use the word *mystery*, and she knew to describe the "manners" of a segment of a Georgia county's God-fearing population; and she knew to wonder at God's purpose in putting us here—a philosophical inclination that can prompt everything from revivalism to the writing of stories or essays, Miss O'Connor certainly realized. As for the more "progressive" faith many of us proudly assert, she was not impressed with it: "I have just got back from the Symposium on Religion and Art at Sweet Briar and boy do I have a stomach full of liberal religion! The Devil had his day there!" The words were addressed to her dear friends Sally and Robert Fitzgerald (1963). She sustained a complex relationship between her intellectual and religious life. She read widely, was personally no stranger to a number of liberal intellectuals. Yet, she repeatedly avowed religious "orthodoxy." She connected what goes wrong with what is sinful—God's judgment, or His terribly hard-to-fathom ways. She was not one, that is, to overlook the workings of original sin in our lives. "Ideal Christianity doesn't exist," she wrote a nun friend, "because anything the human being touches, even Christian truth, he deforms slightly in his own image." She added for emphasis that "even the saints do this." She explained: "I take it to be the effects of Original Sin, and I notice that Catholics often act as if that doctrine is always perverted and always an indication of Calvinism." As for her obligation: "The writer has to make the corruption believable before he can make the grace meaningful."

That she surely tried to do—with a light touch so that the gravest matters would not become too forbidding to her mostly secular readers. When she observed to an anonymous correspondent (1963) that she would even postpone her work an hour in order to see on television W. C. Fields in "Never Give a Sucker an Even Break," she is indicating how much she loved to laugh, and how important she believed the connection between humor and a certain kind of everyday grace that the Lord gives His people as they trudge those long, long journeys toward Jerusalem. (That movie's title, rather obviously, might have one day been the title for a story of Miss O'Connor's: it has the sound, the shape of one of her titles—meant to mock sententious aphorisms, even biblical pieties.) And she understood that humor was a vehicle for the deliverance of a kind of seriousness otherwise shunned by many of today's readers. Through humor she could bring us closer to the religious passions of those fellow southerners she herself not only peopled her stories with, but thought about consistently and with considerable intelligence.

In a letter to her friend Sister Mariella Gable, Miss O'Connor took on the charge that she was drawn in her fiction to strange and "fanatic" people. She is more subtle, I think, than a battalion of social psychiatrists in the way she observes the normative element in psychological appraisal, whether done by a social scientist, a reader, a critic:

People make a judgment of fanaticism by what they are themselves. To a lot of Protestants I know, monks and nuns are fanatics, none greater. And to a lot of the monks and nuns I know, my Protestant prophets are fanatics. For my part, I think the only difference between them is that if you are a Catholic and have this intensity of belief you join the convent and are heard from no more; whereas if you are a Protestant and have it, there is no convent for you to join and you go about in the world getting into all sorts of trouble and drawing the wrath of people who don't believe anything much at all down on your head. This is one reason why I can write about Protestant believers better than Catholic believers—because they express their belief in diverse kinds of dramatic action which is obvious enough for me to catch.

In her stories that phrase "intensity of belief" is something her various characters already have, or find growing in themselves, and it is something they often simply don't know what to do with. In this secular world, such "intensity" goes elsewhere—into politics, psychology, or the self as an object of obsessive concern, passion, veneration. In the South, still, there are men and women whose "intensity" remains religious throughout their lives. And they are usually not the urban churchgoers—though anyone who has lived up North and goes South even to Atlanta or Charlotte or Birmingham, is bound to notice how many more churches are available to people, rich and middle-class and poor, and how much better attended are those southern churches. But O'Connor's religiously haunted, if not pursued men and women are not really churchgoers; they are souls who lust for God, who crave Him, who seek Him with a singleness of purpose that is called "fanatic" up North, or in southern centers of sophistication.

In contrast, other forms of ardent pursuit or affiliation are accepted by many of us as in no manner surprising or exceptional. A black woman we knew in Mississippi, an inveterate revivalist herself, a person always getting "calls" from "Christ the Lord," had occasion to view for a summer (during the Mississippi Project of 1964) activities and involvements of young white and black civil rights activists. Now, some fifteen years later, all that soldiering, as she called it, has disappeared, has gone elsewhere:

I used to watch those people, and I'd think to myself that they were doing the work of the Lord, of Christ the Lord. But I began to see that they weren't worrying about God; they were worried about us—and they weren't forgetting themselves, either. The colored folks of Itta Bena and Louise and Midnight, right here in the state of Mississippi—we were important because we were part of their big plans to change the world. They'd come up to us, and they'd want us to sign something, and they'd want us to come to their meetings, and when we came, they had talks to give us, speeches—long sermons. They'd try to be more upset than we were! There's no one more upset about the way the white people treat us folks here than we are. We've been trying to get the white man off our backs for a long time. He's on our backs the way some white folks are on the backs of other white folks. You'd have to own the federal army to change all that! Don't you think we know who has the guns and the billy-clubs and who hasn't got them; and who has all the money, and who hasn't. If you have money, you have the police on your side, and the soldiers. If you're on top, there's not a thing anyone can do to touch you. Those civil rights people didn't think we knew that. They'd tell us what we already knew, and they'd love hearing themselves talk. They kept saying we're all soldiers in a big important war.

You bet we are; you bet we're soldiers. We're all going to die; and some of us will go to meet the Lord, and some of us will "descend into hell," it says in the Book. But we have our General, and if we'd only stay loyal to Him, we'd turn around the whole world. Since we don't stay loyal, the only thing to hope for is the next world, when we'll have a second chance. You'd tell your faith to the civil rights folks, and they'd look down at the ground, and they'd wait you out, with a bad, bad look in their eyes, and their mouths turned down, and they'd be scratching the back of their necks, until you've stopped talking, so they could start talking. And boy, did they talk! I told one white boy from up there in Massachusetts that he's going to be a minister of Christ the Lord one of these days, when he sees the light. But he didn't like what I said, no he didn't. He just went on, telling me what I should be, and telling me about the heaven we're going to have here in this country, if only we'd turn everything around.

Well, there's no heaven but in Heaven. And if you don't know that, you don't know much. That's what I believe. Of course, you can't tell some poeple much. They want to tell *you everything*. That's how it goes: they come here to help us, but oh, if we don't bow and scrape to their every idea, then they lose patience with us, and I declare, you see them looking at you no different than the sheriff, and the people at the post office, and like that. Scratch some of the white civil rights people and you have the plantation owners. Scratch some of the black civil rights people, and you have the white talkers. And Lord, they talked! They could be so sure of themselves! I went to their Freedom House in Canton. My sister took me. They were arguing, and they were telling each other that *this* is right and *that* is right, and after awhile I thought to myself that here, if you're colored or white, and God calls you, then you read His book, and you try to do what He wants of you. But these people, they didn't read the Bible. They read a lot; but they didn't read the Bible. They read a lot about what people say about them—the newspapers. They read the books of their own people—the professors who taught them. They had pictures up, of their friends and their family, and that man from India or someplace. They had stories to tell you about the troubles they were having here in Mississippi. They sounded like our Lord Himself, all the burdens they took on their shoulders. You don't know how bad life is here, until you hear them preaching at you! I guess they're right. Lord knows, they're right. But it's us living here, not them. It's us who will stay here and stay here, until the Lord calls for us.

It's your own life you should live. When you start living another person's life, you lose your own, and you mix up the other person's. That's how I see it. My grandma used to tell us that a good person is one who knows how much trouble she has, and tries to do the best she can, and a bad person is someone who's always telling other people how much trouble they've got themselves in, and how they should follow him, and he'll get them out of it. Follow the Lord. Some of these people, who came down here, they believed in men, not angels; and sure enough, they didn't believe in God. It's their choice; but it might have been nice if they'd said to me: it's your choice. Instead, they felt sorry for us. Jesus Christ didn't feel sorry for the people He went and attended to. He loved them. He healed them out of love. He wanted them on their feet and the equal of other people. He didn't want them to pray to other people; He wanted them to thank God. On your knees to Him; "yes, sir," and "yes, ma'am" to the white folks, and hello to your colored brethren, but to God Almighty, it's a prayer, and it's please, dear Lord, please, and I've failed again. There's a big difference between Him and us, that's for sure. And if you follow Him, if you really do, then there's a big difference between yourself and your neighbor, that's for sure, too.

In fairness, many of the young people she felt grateful to, curious about, and more than a bit impatient with, were seeking what Flannery O'Connor considered so important—an institution, a "movement," a commitment, that would both give direction to their particular "intensities," and set limits on them. For that black woman religious fervor was as natural as a long, long Delta afternoon. She was able to recognize other kinds of fervor easily because she knew enough about herself to understand her own kind. She realized that those young activists were not as unlike her as they may have thought.

She was, as Miss O'Connor put it, trying to "go about in the world" —praying hard and working hard and worrying hard. Fear, always fear: the white man, sure of himself and fickle. But hope, always hope: a God immediate and accessible. She was not a black to go knocking on any church door, for the sake of integration. She was a black who wanted to vote and see school integration, but shunned some of the rhetoric of the time, because she sensed in it fanaticism. Not the fanaticism of a Klan or a racist mob; yet, fanaticism: "They think they're going to bring God's Kingdom down here to the Delta tomorrow, and they are wrong, wrong."She is not to be taken, in that observation, as a reactionary, as a hopelessly passive, inert, superstitious person—one with an all too convenient outlook, so far as the status quo goes. She is no fool politically. And no bad prophet; she saw (right off, in 1963) how soon it would be that the civil rights movement was over, and her neighbors and she would be, once again, on their own completely. She also saw the hunger in her well-intentioned, decent liberators. Some of them had, back then, the "wrath" toward her that Flannery O'Connor mentions—a resentment of a faith that seemed so very strong and imperturable. But there was a touch of envy in their hearts, and she knew it. How could people, severely rebuked and scorned, hold their heads so uncannily high, even when yessing endlessly the "principalities and powers?" And the more negatively those people were viewed, the more feverishly they were hectored, the more inscrutable, stubborn, hard to deal with they became: strangely acting religious "fanatics."

The issue, Flannery O'Connor realized full well, is one's point of view. For her, the "fanatics" she approached through stories were "crypto-Catholic" in nature—prophets out of the South's rural life who felt the strong pull of the Holy Ghost, and used the words of the Holy Bible. For her, Southern Evangelical Protestantism was, unmistakably, a religion of the poor, those low down on all the ladders that a measurement conscious society constructs. When she was creating a prophet, she was taking up the subject of justice and injustice, Evil and its daily victories, Good and the constant losses it suffers—and Christ as, again, the Incarnation of some of those abstractions, or as the Incarnation of the Divine Antagonist to others of those abstractions. These humble southerners, these dirt-poor men and women, scorned nationally, and sometimes scorned regionally, too, have had every reason to search the skies and ask why. Why their fate—not only their material fate, but their fate at the hands of their judges?

Small wonder they have turned their backs on those who would patronize them, or invite them to come in, once a week, Sunday late morning, for a bit of friendly prayer. Small wonder they would embrace a Lord who went directly to His people, and promises them that in some future moment the whole rotten edifice of exploitation and snobbery and arrogance and condescension will come tumbling down. And for us outsiders, out of our own fanaticism, to mistake such a radical religion as an "opiate" or an "illusion" is to reveal at the least a willful ignorance. Theirs is a country, spiritual radicalism that denounces the rich. A radicalism addressed to the poor. A radicalism that stresses an egalitarian hope. A radicalism that is unsurprised by the betrayal of any earthly plan or project at the hands of egoism, envy, rivalry, and so on. A radicalism, actually, that has read rather correctly this particular century's various messianic secular creeds, and their social or cultural or political expressions.

In her essay "The Teaching of Literature," Flannery O'Connor told her readers that a man had once sent her a message through her uncle: "Tell that girl to quit writing about poor folks." That particular man had a reason for his annoyance: "I see poor folks every day and get mighty tired of them, and when I read, I don't want to see any more of them." There may well be, for some, a different kind of objection. "I am against poverty," the message goes, "and the sooner we get rid of it the better. But these 'poor people' of Flannery O'Connor's are a strange bunch; they don't seem to know how bad off they are. It's pie in the sky for them, and no matter if the belly goes empty, day in and day out. And as kooks, with strange preoccupations, they take the reader's attention away from the objective circumstances of their lives, which are slighted in the descriptions of who they are and how they live." I borrow from a criticism written by one of my Harvard students about the "themes" that run through Miss O'Connor's "Complete Stories."

In fact, she was an author who took care to observe closely "the manners of the poor." She concluded, correctly, I believe, that the poor she had so observed, the South's poor, "love formality"; and that, furthermore, "the mystery of existence is always showing through the texture of their ordinary lives." She also added the obvious—that "the poor live with less padding between them and the raw forces of life." But she knew that the result was not necessarily, as some of their self-appointed protectors and defenders assert, a deracinated, superstitious, gullible, apathetic lumpenproletariat; or in the South, a Klan-infested collection of ignorant, coarse rednecks.

The poor for her are limited, yes—prone to know hurt, loss, frustration, a sense of uncertainty, if not despair. One is emphatically not romanticizing poverty or making light of its hardships by pointing out, as she did repeatedly, that there is a connection, existential if you will, between such emotions, as experienced among Georgia's or Louisiana's "poor white trash," or "colored folks" working as tenants, and emotions the rest of us have all the time—or if we don't, are in more trouble than we know. It is to the glory of any number of tenant farmers, or small-town working people of the South that they have realized precisely what Miss O'Connor has them realizing about themselves and their condition. A desperate poverty can prompt two kinds of hunger: physical hunger with an accompanying exasperation and sadness; spiritual hunger is a response to that exasperation, that sadness.

"Why do we have this life, and they have their life?" A question of a ten-year-old black child; I heard it asked in New Orleans toward the end of 1960, when all the craziness of segregationist defiance had spilled onto the streets of that supposedly sophisticated old port city. The child had racial distinctions in mind, understandably. Why were blacks confined, whites in complete charge of everything, it seemed? But the longer one spends with such a child, the more one hears her move—a moment here, a bit longer than a moment there—to those larger questions that are commonly claimed the province of theologians. And how many of our developmental psychologists, or our psychiatrists, insist that a child called "mature," let alone an adult simularly categorized, ask the morally reflective questions she posed to herself and others? "I wonder when they hiss at me and call me 'nigger,' and 'nigger girl,' and 'animal,' why they do that," she said—a few days before a bleak, scary Christmas. She tried hard for an explanation:

I remember what the minister told us—that Jesus went through the same thing, and the reason was, He knew a lot of us would be going through something like that, before we go and die, and meet Him. They hung Him on the Cross, because they couldn't stand that He was a good, good man. I guess they shout at us because they can't stand that we're trying to do a little good, and give the colored the same chance as the white.

If the whites really had a good life, they wouldn't be so bad to us. We're only here this one time, and we have to prove ourselves. The people in the mob, they're proving themselves. It's too bad. My momma says the Devil has gone and taken them. I see the Devil in their faces. They're mean people. They've been kicked bad, or they wouldn't be so mean. One woman said so many bad things to me that I wanted to cry. If I wasn't afraid, I'd have stopped and prayed to Jesus, right to her face! My grandma told me to do that, but my daddy said no. And I'm sure the police would have stopped me, and told me to hurry on, and so would the federal marshals they have going with us.

I think of that woman, screaming at me, and I wonder who she is. What will God do, when she comes before Him to be judged? What will He say to her? That's what my grandmother wants to know. But God won't tell us. Maybe He wants us to find out for ourselves. But we don't know how to find out. Maybe we're here to find out—to find out what the matter is with that white woman and her girl. That girl isn't much older than me, and she calls me bad names, too. She and her mother may both be sending themselves to the Devil, like my grandma says. But why? Will God try to save her, like He did all the people, when He came here on earth to visit?"

The motions of fear. The motions of charity. The motions of human inquiry. "In the gospels," Flannery O'Connor wrote, "it was the devils who first recognized Christ, and the evangelists didn't censor this information. They apparently thought it was pretty good witness. It scandalizes us when we see the same thing in modern dress only because we have this defensive attitude toward faith." A black child, under extreme duress, was groping her way toward that realization. Why shouldn't enemies know one another right off? And was that not why Christ talked about coming "to send not peace, but a sword?" The complacency and self-sufficiency, the smug piety of much of contemporary religion, Protestant or Catholic, vexed Miss O'Connor no end. Her story "A Good Man Is Hard To Find," which so titillated some critics and aroused the disdain of others, and confirmed for many her reputation as someone who glorifies violence, or is all too comfortable with the freakish bearers of it, was, in fact, an effort to show, dramatically, how encrusted most of us are in (deathly) secular pieties—in ourselves and our all jazzed-up and catered-to "needs." The advertising slogans that kill us, the various customs and habits that kill us, the kind of dreary, self-indulgent thinking that kills us are, in turn, challenged by the arrival of a Bible-haunted "Misfit," who kills the very people T. S. Eliot, more solemnly, and without the drama of a lively storyteller, described as "hollow," as "stuffed," as possessed of "dried voices" as, collectively, "headpiece filled with straw." To rage at straw, to want to burn it, or slash away at it, to create characters similarly alarmed and disgusted, is not to be a "devil" of a writer, but to have a notion of what devils there are among us—and how firm their hold is, hence the violence of the struggle, if one is to be waged.

Much of the incredulity Miss O'Connor's fiction prompts (who are these strange, wild, raging folk, many of them talking religion and more religion?) is precisely what she expected, and, maybe, wanted. Incredulity is a lack of belief; and she knew her audience on that score rather well. Her situation was not unlike that of many black and white southerners who have found themselves challenged by outsiders: How do I get across what I believe in, when I am speaking to people—dear friends or earnest foes—who don't have either my eyes or my ears, or a received tradition anything like the one I have? No wonder she went after even (maybe, especially) her "Catholic critics"—who were, she had good reason to believe, "crypto-secularists," or "crypto-American pietists," if I may draw upon a way we had of putting things. She wished they would have given her a bit more leeway. She wished they might have recognized in her intentions (to use a phrase of hers) a "sort of 'inscape' as Hopkins would have had it." She had little patience with her coreligionists who wanted to ape other unqualified optimists and meliorists of our time with a notion of life as something to be "actualized," as something full of "real experiences," as something that will get better and better with a bout of exercise, a sexual technique, a "group experience," a social program, a political reform, a few friends made and people influenced. As in "better living through chemistry." Or is it nuclear physics? Or "insight psychotherapy," along with the application of lessons gained from "psychohistory" to our society?

At one point in her career (1957) she had this terribly important and revealing comment to offer anyone who wanted to know about what it was that she kept in mind as she set her characters forth on their journeys, and so doing, continued on her own quite special one: "St. Cyril of Jerusalem, in instructing catechumens, wrote: 'The dragon sits by the side of the road, watching those who pass. Beware lest he devour you. We go to the Father of Souls, but it is necessary to pass by the dragon.' She would never tell a story, write a novel, without tapping her readers forcefully on the shoulder with that message, worked into country talk, country description, country manners. The displaced person became for both Mrs. Shortley and Mrs. McIntyre such a dragon. Hazel Motes met his fair share of dragons in Taulkinham. And poor Parker found in his wife such a dragon. No one whom Miss O'Connor created and spent a lot of time and labor on would be spared that dragon. How could they, if they were to be taken seriously by her, and she hoped, by those who responded to her comic seriousness, her unfailing determination to collar her readers and, it can be said, confront them with dragons—her stories? By that, I mean an intention of shock not for its own sake, but in the sense of a challenge, a confrontation, a reminder, a rebuff: here is what you have come to, what we all face coming to, unless we stop and ask where we are going, and unless we stop and look around and realize what dragon it is that may already be upon us, or have us in its throat, if not well within its stomach.

Even the titles of her stories tell us the road she walked, a southern version of our twentieth-century one, but recognizable (she always knew) in the North or the West: "A Stroke of Good Fortune"; "The Life You Save May Be Your Own"; "You Can't Be Any Poorer Than Dead"; "A Good Man Is Hard to Find"—sayings that have to do with success and failure, but also with the ultimates of human experience, life and death. What we consider to be "good fortune," the kind of life we want to live, and thereby, save for others, or for God upon Judgment Day (if we are inclined to think that way), the search for goodness, and the ironies of that search, the absurdities, the surprises, the strange pleasures or discontents—all of that is the stuff of her fiction. And all of that is essentially of a religious nature, she both knew and believed.

The quote she offered from St. Cyril is not an easy one for many of us to hear, let alone to accept. We are used to getting rid of difficulties, clearing the road of any obstacles, annoyances, whatever. Planning! Modern techniques! Knowledge is Power! Bulldozers Away! No wonder she called upon the instructions a Christian saint gave to his catechumens. No doubt she regarded herself and a good number of the rest of us as ones badly in need of receiving such instruction in the doctrines of Christianity. And none are more needy, she kept saying, than the intellectuals of the United States of America, be they of the northern variety, or her own southern kind. It was for her a vexing issue, a serious and recurring problem: the mind of modern man. What have the imperatives of that mind, all caught up in various secular ideologies and faiths, come to mean for us, as we proceed not by step on dusty, primitive, rutted roads toward Jerusalem, but at a clip in our automobiles on the variously numbered interstates? She would not stop, to the end of her life, asking that question—in her letters, in her written and spoken essays, in her fiction. Nor would her audience fail to get the prickly, unnerving, sometimes accusing message. It is necessary to take seriously what came to be an "affair" of sorts: Flannery O'Connor and her passionately insistent involvement with people of her own (intellectual) kind, if not, commonly, her own faith.

THREE

A SOUTHERN INTELLECTUAL

IN 1957 FLANNERY O'CONNOR wrote Granville Hicks a letter in response to his request that she contribute to a symposium he was editing, to be called *The Living Novel*. She sent him a carefully prepared talk she had recently delivered at a college. The talks were, in fact, essays, which she read. (Some of them would eventually become part of *Mystery and Manners*.) She ends her letter to Hicks rather assertively: "I'm not an intellectual and have a horror of making an idiot of myself with abstract statements and theories." And a few months before death finally claimed her, she was unrelenting on the matter. Yet again she resorted to a deliberate spelling mistake that had served a prejudice for many years: "I think of you often," she told her friend Richard Stern, "in that cold place among them interleckchuls." The "place" is the University of Chicago, and the man she is writing to, a teacher, a novelist, a person of obvious cultural refinement. And so was she: a wonderfully strict, demanding lecturer, who had scant patience with sloppy or fuzzy minds; a brilliant short-story writer and novelist, who worked all kinds of theological and philosophical subtleties into the structure of her tales; and not least, as her recently published correspondence especially reveals, a woman of extraordinary intellectual depth, with a hungry mind that was willing to travel widely and deeply. She steeped herself in literature, of course; religion, of course; but also history and art and psychology and, in her own sharp fashion, the South's social and political matters.

Nor are those relatively informal remarks, made in letters, exceptional moments of pique. If one turns to her collected nonfiction there are repeated jabs at social science, psychology, theorists, and by only the slightest of indirection, the entire liberal, secular world—members of which, she never forgot, made up the overwhelming majority of her readers. She quotes Pascal, for instance, with obvious relish; she describes herself as a writer who takes quite seriously his advice that one should believe in the "God of Abraham, Isaac, Jacob and not of the philosophers and scholars." She scorns readers who once wanted a moral lesson out of fiction but "now feel they have to drain off a statable social theory that will make life more worth living." And in her many references to the South, whose virtues she championed relentlessly, and at a time—the fifties and early sixties—when the region was under sustained moral and political attack, she was quick to make the states of the Old Confederacy a refuge of sorts for a certain kind of anti-intellectual. In an enumeration, for example, of what she loved about her homeland, she referred to the strong religious tradition, the sobering experience of defeat and violation (which make for a tragic sensibility), and then added: "a distrust of the abstract, a sense of dependence on the grace of God, and a knowledge that evil is not simply a problem to be solved, but a mystery to be endured."

Nor would she let the matter rest there—with a blunt criticism of the social meliorism that has worked its way into the assumptions of many twentieth-century educated Westerners. In a description of the opportunities open to the Catholic novelist who lives in the South, she uses the personal pronoun *he*, but is unmistakably referring to herself when she says: "I think he will feel a good deal more kinship with backwoods prophets and shouting fundamentalists than he will with those politer elements for whom the supernatural is an embarrassment and for whom religion has become a department of sociology or culture or personality development." In the same vein, and the same lecture, she spoke of "the logic that kills" and of those who are in the habit of "making categories smaller and smaller"—clear thrusts at a certain kind of intellectual mind.

Her correspondence, only available to us in 1979, fifteen years after her death, is even more interesting in its consistent mixture of intellectual depth and anti-intellectual sentiment, the latter sometimes acid in tone, other times humorously rendered. I have already referred to some letters she sent. For a woman who never allowed herself to get swept up in social or political causes, who was sick, actually, when the South's turmoil began to take place, and who died before it reached a climax, Miss O'Connor could be, at times, sharply egalitarian. She knew that many writers and academics were rather too instantly and noisily ready to support distant, just causes, while maintaining for themselves, nearer at home, all sorts and conditions of privilege. To an anonymous friend she remarks: "I have no notion that the artist should be above the common people; the question is who are the common people now? I confess I don't know. . . . I even dislike the concept *artist* when it sets you above, all it is is working in a certain kind of medium to make something right. The material is no more exalted than any other kind of material and the idea of making it right is what should be applied to all making."

At times in her letters she took pains to associate herself with people she wasn't at all like. She might misspell the word *intellectual* (as above) to tease a friend who was one—and not necessarily a Yankee. She had her share of southern intellectual friends, and she could be openly provocative with them—as if she had to deflate herself and the person with whom she was exchanging letters, lest they both be accused, by her rather sensitive and strong-minded conscience, of being snobbish. "First time I had been to the picter show in two or three years," she wrote to one such Georgia friend. "It was not such a bad picture," she continued, now resuming a correct spelling, "but I ain't going again for another three years if I can possibly help it." And to the Fitzgeralds, in a joking aside, she referred to her "poor white trash look." But she was more seriously alarmed by certain intellectual or cultural trends, be they of northern origin or not; and she was quite anxious to dissociate herself from them, if not parody them, ridicule them, or pray hard for those captivated if not captured by them. Here she is going after a representative moment in American educational life: "I lectured at Wesleyan College in Macon last year and as a result some of their students who have a vague urge to 'express themselves' began to come regularly to see me. When they appear, they do all the talking and they have fantastic but very positive ideas about how everything is and ought to be; and they are mighty sophisticated on the outside. The visits leave me exhausted and yearning to go sit with the chickens."

The last sentence is, of course, the most devastating of all—a mock escape from unacknowledged pretension and foolishness to honest, down-to-earth nature. Sometimes, in her exchanges, the South becomes such a refuge—a place where the chic and the trendy of Manhattan or California or wherever have not yet penetrated. But she was too honest and experienced an observer to be able to have it that way for long. Her own life, lived in Savannah and Milledgeville, told her otherwise: "Anything having to do with this 'learning from life' stuff turns my stomach permanently. I had to attend a 'progressive' high school here, one of those connected with a teachers' college. In the summer all the teachers went to T.C. and sat at the feet of an old boy named William Heard Kilpatrick. In the winter they returned and asked us what, as mature children, we thought we ought to study. At that school we were always 'planning.' They would as soon have given us arsenic in the drinking fountains as let us study Greek. I know no history whatsoever."

A bit harsh, one suspects. She certainly knew her history. She knew her grammar, too, though at moments she wouldn't allow so. When she and her mother sent a Christmas fruitcake to their good friends Sally and Robert Fitzgerald, then living in Italy, a letter from the victim of Teachers College educational modernism observed, worriedly, that she "would hate for some Eye-talian to getaholt to it sometime" before the recipients did. Pure jest. Or maybe, an American greeting, southern dialect style, to some dear, temporary expatriates. As for her advice to Elizabeth and Robert Lowell (in 1957) that it "is not good to raise a child in Boston [because] they think anybody who didn't go to Harvard or MIT is underprivileged," she was once more indulging herself with a rather conventional barb—a way to show her good, folksy concern for their daughter's future. On the other hand, are we to dismiss the following as merely a cranky aside, written in a bad mood, and at the prospect of a tiring lecture trip to faraway Lansing, Michigan (1956)? "She allows there are many interesting young writers and intellectuals there that I will enjoy meeting," a friend is told. And then the punch line: "Anything I can't stand it's a young writer or intellectual." This from a writer of thirty-one, just coming into her own; and a woman of serious introspection, with the broadest and deepest of reading habits.

She would scorn, and properly so, the simple-minded explanations for such an apparent paradox; explanations that exhort through words such as *ambivalence*, or phrases such as *the problems of the southern woman*. To be sure, she lived in a South, in an America for that matter, not yet willing to examine thoroughly the way women are encouraged toward or discouraged from particular jobs, vocations, interests. Still, there is no small tradition, among southern women, of writing as a sanctioned choice of occupation. She knew Katherine Anne Porter, Cecil Dawkins. She admired Eudora Welty. She disliked Carson McCullers' work but read it. And she knew and liked such Yankee writers as Elizabeth Bishop and Elizabeth Hardwick. Her mother, her kin, her neighbors may not have appreciated her work in the manner of the critics who examined it for the literary quarterlies, but there was certainly no embarrassment in connection with her obviously well-received stories or novels. Admittedly, there are no great salons in Baldwin County; and there has always been a certain skepticism of Yankee (or southern) intellectuals in parts of the rural South (or the urban South, or the rural North, or even, vast stretches of the urban North). All intellectuals struggle with the suspicion, resentment, envy of various fellow citizens, fellow human beings, whereas only some move back and forth, now talking as confident, discerning critics of ideas, books, events, now as irate critics of—their own kind. Of course, the psychological explanations for anti-intellectualism are always inviting these days: a masochism; an anxiety about one's purpose or abilities, converted into an aggressive position toward others, the possible judges; a chronic ambivalence with respect to one's hopes and ambitions; in sum, a variety of personal "problems" and, no doubt, a social sensitivity that accurately gauges and responds to the mix of respect and resentment many intellectuals stimulate in people.

The problem with that line of reasoning is that it ends up turning a self-critical intellectual disposition into a matter of psychopathology. And the trouble with *that* is, quite simply, that anyone's relationship to anything can be similarly (that is, psychiatrically) approached, so that the issues becomes, basically, a normative one. For instance, the willing and enthusiastic intellectual, of the southern or Yankee variety, can also be analyzed with respect to his or her motivations: fear, anxiety, covetousness, hostility, and the rest—universals of human experience. What was Flannery O'Connor quite consciously and rationally struggling with, when she took positions, seriously argued or through humorous asides, in seeming opposition to particular modes of thinking, regarded (by many of us, at least) as "intellectual" in nature? She gave us a hint in a stern, reproving letter to her friend William Sessions. He had found difficulties with her novel *The Violent Bear It Away*, had communicated them to her, and so doing, had obviously aroused her ire. "You see everything in terms of sex symbols," she told him, and pointedly added, "and in a way that would not enter my head—the lifted bough, the fork of the trees, the corkscrew." Then she went to the heart of her objection: "It doesn't seem to be conceivable to you that such things merely have a natural place in the story, a natural use."

She was making a storyteller's plea for the integrity of everyday life—its realities, its movement, its drama, its textures, its things. The apparent is, after all, the apparent; even if there are undercurrents in this life. And one use of art is to survey what things look like, sound like—a mighty demanding job, and one that ought be respected on its own merits. Nor would she be interested in an "interpretation" which claims that because those "sex symbols" didn't "enter" her "head," does not mean they aren't there, to be remarked by a critic such as her correspondent. No one, of course, not even the writer who creates a story, a novel, can tell others what to get out of their reading. But a writer has his or her obligation to make clear a particular intent; and Miss O'Connor was not unwilling to do just that—and go a step further: ask why certain others missed what she sincerely felt herself to be about, in favor of discoveries that struck her as—well: "Your criticism sounds to me as if you have read too many critical books and are too smart in an artificial, destructive, and very limited way."

She goes on at some length, tries to explain just what she had in mind with her novel. She was not out to give an arrogant or condescending back of her hand to a reader she disagreed with. She was clearly upset that her essentially religious interests, provided a southern, rural setting, were not really being attended, not even considered worth much notice. Why, she wondered, would the "spirit of the book" be overlooked, in favor of a study of its psychoanalytic imagery? She knew the answer, without question: a steep decline in interest in religion, during this century, among so-called "thinking people," many of whom use psychology or economics or political theory as the only "interesting" way of looking at believers, at what they believe, or at those who urge belief—independently (evangelical preachers), or in the name of institutions (her own Catholic Church, its priests, nuns, bishops).

No question, she could slip from such a position of frustration or hurt into a more personal kind of pique—though not without resort, usually, to a good deal of accompanying reason. "I do hope," she told her friend, "that you will get over the kind of thinking that sees in every door handle a phallic symbol and that ascribes such intentions to those who have other fish to fry. The Freudian technique can be applied to anything at all with equally ridiculous results. The fork of the tree! My Lord, Billy, recover your simplicity. You ain't in Manhattan. Don't inflict that stuff on the poor students there; they deserve better." After which she mentioned looking forward to seeing Mr. Sessions on Thanksgiving Day!

She sometimes resorted to self-critical irony—a measure, perhaps, of the distance she felt between herself and a Manhattan she knew to be a genuine center of literary culture. Some of her dearest friends lived there, or near there, and so had she, until sickness took her home. Once back South, she kept her eyes and ears open. She tells Mr. Sessions how very much she has come to rely upon her country neighbors. Their lives, their religious ideas and ideals became important elements in her stories. But such lives, such religious preoccupations, don't interest many urban intellectuals. She felt she wasn't being taken seriously by people whose intelligence she had no reason to doubt. A number of critics insisted on ignoring not only what she had in mind (*religious* symbols) but what she was trying to be: "Hawthorne said he didn't write novels, he wrote romances; I am one of his descendents." That was in the same letter to Mr. Sessions—an almost plaintive, if strong-minded effort to make clear her primary interest in adventure, in surprising incidents, in a dramatic representation of external reality. When she felt misrepresented in her intentions, she could turn sour. In a letter to another friend, written within a week of the one just mentioned, she talks about going to the Piggly Wiggly, about a monthly chicken feed bill of $9.95, about her plans to "tellum this and that" in a forthcoming lecture—and about her sense of herself, at least at that writing: "The letters from the Deans are very intelligent and the head of the English Dept. at one of them has written a book called *The Metaphoric Tradition in Modern Poetry*, it being a study of Auden, Jarrell, Williams (William Carlos) and Stevens. I feel very Country Bumpkinish in such society."

Maybe we owe it to her not to make too much of such a remark. Even the most talented, sophisticated mind (and hers was both) is entitled to a confessional moment of self-doubt. But her modesty did take a somewhat truculent form. At the same time, she could fall back upon a form of self-definition that wasn't altogether accurate. She came from an old, aristocratic, well-to-do family. She received an excellent education, despite her polemics against part of it. And with respect to William Carlos Williams, certainly, it is ironic to hear such an avowal on her part. He, too, in *Paterson*, in his *Autobiography* and in *his* correspondence, was constantly inclined to denigrate himself as a country doctor. Like her, he was concerned with the concrete ("no ideas but in things"), and insistently antiacademic. His symbolic Manhattan was, of course, England, where T. S. Eliot had chosen to live —though he was not beyond a suspicion of the real Manhattan. He might have had a flourishing practice there: the "writers and intellectuals" Miss O'Connor once lumped together in an angry moment. But he preferred to stay with *his* people—the North's "poor white trash," from whom he learned so much, and whom he often pitted against the American and English Cambridges. His example ought to caution us not to make too much of the *southern* element in O'Connor's anti-intellectualism. Even for a northern writer, living right across the river from Manhattan, it is quite possible to feel misunderstood, patronized, unfairly approached—and, not least, a victim of specific or nameless, faceless opponents, all subsumed (sometimes unfairly, perhaps) under designations such as *the academy*, or *the secular critics*.

Perhaps the angriest letter Flannery O'Connor ever wrote (and she was a genuinely gracious person, with exemplary manners—naturally, rather than obsessively, obsequiously or imperiously displayed) was "to a Professor of English," as the person is described in *The Habit of Being*. She begins bluntly: "The interpretation of your ninety students and three teachers is fantastic and about as far from my intentions as it could get to be. If it were a legitimate interpretation, the story would be little more than a trick and its interest would be simply for abnormal psychology. I am not interested in abnormal psychology." She then tries to tell what she was interested in when she wrote "A Good Man Is Hard To Find." For two paragraphs she is her own interpreter —patient, consistent, matter-of-fact, yet also analytic. But she turns stern and reproachful (and eloquent, and a social critic of our time) toward the end, as she moves away from her writing: "The meaning of a story should go on expanding for the reader the more he thinks about it, but meaning cannot be captured in an interpretation. If teachers are in the habit of approaching a story as if it were a research problem for which any answer is believable so long as it is not obvious, then I think students will never learn to enjoy fiction. Too much interpretation is certainly worse than too little, and where feeling for a story is absent, theory will not supply it." For a conclusion she offers one sentence that declares an intention through a negative, and another that was, of course not literally true: "My tone is not meant to be obnoxious. I am in a state of shock."

That is tough talk, by anyone's standards. And it is talk not exactly meant to win critical friends and influence critical people, academic or journalistic or the mixture of the two that gets called "literary." No doubt the author would have thought twice about sending off such comments to a magazine. And, actually, as one reads the letter that prompted such a response (supplied in italics by the editor, Sally Fitzgerald) one begins to wonder whether, maybe, this was a case of the proverbial straw falling upon a Milledgeville back already burdened with errant, wrong-headed explications. The English professor, after all, takes pains to express his admiration for the story, and, really, to ask for her help. But he had touched upon a raw nerve. "The appearance of the Misfit is not 'real,'" he says; but is rather an "illusion or reverie." For Miss O'Connor such a way of looking at her story is not only "psychological" in the sense she remarks upon, but in the broader (or cultural) sense of modern psychology: a way of looking at everyone and everything—not just a manifestly "disturbed" person. She has given no indication that any of the people in her vacationing family are "sick," "demented," prone to hallucinatory experiences. She has given every indication that these are people all too in touch with social reality. They are doing every banal, dreary thing that the rest of us do: eating the food, traveling the roads, witnessing the signs and slogans that, in sum, reveal what *our* illusions and reveries amount to: indulge yourself, divert yourself, amuse yourself, no matter at whose expense, including your own.

When the Misfit arrives, Miss O'Connor has made clear in *Mystery and Manners*, and in a number of her letters, he is expected to be treated by the reader, at the very least, with the same order of credibility accorded all the other characters in the story. However, in a letter the author is told that such has not been the case. All right: why the fierce reaction? It was galling for her to find psychology used in such a manner that the self-centered, secular, gimmee culture she was portraying had in its hands an ultimate protective weapon. She had tired of polite compliments, followed by gestures meant to pull the rug out from everything she held so dear. Bailey is the Grandmother's grandson; he is driving the car, and he is the one the professor latches on to: how could an "enlightened" writer (a professing Christian lady!) send a child—well, a hardly grown youth—into the hands of a brutal murderer, along with everyone else in this "innocent" family! A solution: she did no such thing. She is, after all, a twentieth-century novelist, who understands the violence young people feel toward their elders, toward others of their age, toward themselves, and she is ingenious enough with symbols and at narrative to work into a powerful, compelling story a sophisticated, contemporary, psychological view of what happens in the mind—against the background of contemporary American life.

For Miss O'Connor, however, the suggestion that "reality fades," as the professor put it, with the arrival of the Misfit is quite another suggestion: that the liberal, secular sentimentality of our age will brook no interference, even in fictional form. Sex can be used in any way any writer chooses, but not violence. And a Jesus-talking man who ends up killing people, one after the other—how "primitive" can one get! Meanwhile, the terrible violence of everyday life goes on. The violence done people by governments, corporations. The violence that is random, senseless, unremitting it seems. Violence in the name of profit. Violence in the name of greed. Violence in the name of sex. Violence in the name of madness. And, of course, violence in the name of good. The violence of tires that are no good: death on the roads. The violence of the Gulag Archipelago. The violence that our agents, and the agents of our enemies, commit—in the name of national causes, in the name of "America the Beautiful," or the proletariat of the world.

One can go on and on, enumerating the banality of violence—worked into television commercials and State of the Union speeches and addresses to various politbureaus; worked into the sectarianism of "encounter" groups, where people turn on others viciously, arrogantly, self-righteously, in the name of "candor" and something called "psychological awareness"; worked into academic feuds, in which careers become cannon fodder for demanding vanities, for unadmitted meanness in desperate search of expression; and worked into the struggles of all sorts of individuals, some who call themselves "conservative," and unashamedly "wealthy," and some who call themselves "radical," and out only for the interests of their fellow human beings. Paraguay and Cambodia. Finland and Rhodesia. Southern counties and northern ghettoes, well removed from "lily-white" suburbs. Crusades and wars of liberation. Liberty, equality, fraternity—and the guillotine overworked. A worldwide, continuing history of dreams turned into nightmares. Speaking of which: Freud and Jung, colleagues and scholarly friends, become Freudians and Jungians, at one another's necks —maybe not literally, but the words can be pretty vicious, the distortions severe, the grudges unending. Is there really anything scandalous or all that surprising about a story in which a person fueled by passion connected to an idea turns on an all too obvious and available "enemy?"

Miss O'Connor tells the professor, naturally, that she is not depicting Georgia rural life. But why, she must have asked herself, does he worry that she might possess such an intention? She was not responding to her neighbors. She was responding to her knowledge of the Bible, to her faith in the God of Jeremiah and Isaiah, the God whose Son Jesus, "came not to send peace, but a sword," and Who let forth considerable rage in the Temple, and Who Himself was killed—a Misfit of all times sent to a humiliating bloody, public death. But, she had no mind to make the Misfit a "Christ symbol." Who are these people, she must have wondered, who would expect me to have that kind of automatic, pleasingly shocking "symbolism" at my fingertips? If the Misfit had "delivered" the family in some way, had given them a few pieties to remember, and then maybe, for the sake of drama, had united with them against, say, a crowd of murderous Klan members—then Miss O'Connor would have been celebrated (she would have feared) as a wise and thoughtful southerner, as an integrationist, hence brave, compassionate. It was not the kind of approval she sought.

She knew, without the slightest need of Marxist theory, or social science analysis, or Freudian explication, how much violence an apparent civility, an insistently law-abiding mediocrity can conceal. She knew the violence that goes with acquiescence to murderous avarice. Buy products. Do the bidding of various others: travel, dress, eat, and not least, think as they suggest. Think what? The slogans are everywhere. Think hamburgers. Think jeans. Think cars with names such as Dart, Rabbit, Sabre—the last in no way meant to suggest His Sword! Think to consume, but be careful lest others, the saying goes, "rip you off"—speaking of the violence that goes with everyday, "normal" talk, as a reflection of everyday, "normal" life. The Misfit was wildly determined to face down the world's ongoing superficialities, evasions, duplicities. He was wrong-headed in the way he carried out, lived out, the demands of his mind's perceptions and (long yearned for) commitments—the stuff of tragedy. The Misfit's creator wanted his tragedy to be regarded on its own merits. But she had removed herself too far from many of her readers and their preoccupations. And her humor was serious, indeed—as in *The Divine Comedy*.

There is no doubt that Flannery O'Connor's fiction itself often became a battleground. She did not confine her polemics to her essays, her correspondence. A streak of anti-intellectualism runs through the stories, and *The Violent Bear It Away* as well. Some of her most memorable, if not completely successful, characters turn out to be comic versions of psychologists, social workers—individuals whose "liberal humanism" or manifest intellectuality are rather evident. The weak, sad, spiteful, apparently doomed sons of "The Enduring Chill" or "Everything That Rises Must Converge." The willful Hulga, a memorable performance for her creator. The self-conscious Sheppard, anxious to save others, but blind to so much that is happening around him. Rayber of her second novel, a rational, twentieth-century, psychological man. What is the author aiming to tell us, when she confronts these people with their not very promising fates? How well does she succeed—with respect to the credibility of the characters she has created, the stories she has told us? And what dangers does she constantly negotiate, with what success, as she presents us individuals who are, in many ways, ourselves writ large, or, alas, rather small?

"The good thing about the intelligent anti-intellectual," Robert Fitzgerald wrote in 1949 (with regard to William Carlos Williams) "is that he scents with appropriate alarm the dangers of committing himself to abstract attitudes that a later or rougher or rounder experience would show up; he distrusts not only 'those large words that make people unhappy' but all the apparatus of ideas that can get in between us and the things that we do or witness, all stereotypes and, in the extreme case, all stereotypes-to-be." That is a comment Mr. Fitzgerald's friend Flannery O'Connor would scarcely have wanted to take issue with. She was constantly suspicious of the formulations and generalizations that many of us have ceased questioning altogether—have, rather, taken up as our particular Gospel, or, put a bit differently, accepted as the secular Good News this "stage" in civilization has presented to us. If she had a sharp eye out for the rural South's folkways, she was no stranger to the intelligentsia, either the South's, to which she belonged, no matter her protestations, or the Yankee version: colonies of writers, publishing intrigue, critical fashions and reactions to fashions, academic tastes, pro and con, with regard to any number of issues. The letters in *The Habit of Being* show her in constant touch with writers, teachers, people as anxious to share ideas with her, as she was with them. She was an intellectual almost to her last breath, and at the same time she was toughly critical about certain influential intellectual assumptions. Was she, though, susceptible to exaggeration and distortion—the two dangers that commonly accompany such a posture? That is to say, did she overestimate the significance and importance of, say, psychology, in our contemporary life—and give us, at best, only a partially accurate "incarnation" of it, in the persons of Sheppard or Rayber?

She herself worried along those lines. Several times in her correspondence she acknowledges her concern about the way she constructed Rayber. She found it hard to get into his head. She knew she was tempted, in this instance, by caricature. She also knew that to set up a duel for a man's soul, and have one of the antagonists be a straw-man is to risk propaganda: the preachy half-art she cordially detested when she came across it. And maybe, her intellectuals are the weakest element in her fiction—a source of temptation for her, one she tried to avoid, but only with limited success. Yet, each time I read "The Lame Shall Enter First," I am all too sadly reminded of all of us: the child psychiatrists of the twentieth century, evangelist heroes to others, and all too quickly, to ourselves. We believe we know so much. We are going to do so much, rescue so many people, prevail over all sorts of conditions and difficulties. This story of Miss O'Connor's is, in utter brevity, a concrete instance of a constant temptation this life presents: that in trying to gain the whole world we end up lost. It is an account of a psychologist's (or psychiatric social worker's) vigorous, determined effort to "rehabilitate" a boy confined to a reformatory. It is, really, by only the slightest of interpretive extensions or amplifications, an account of professional zeal turned to naught by blindness, incompetence, arrogance—all masquerading as what is, rather too readily, in our time, called "expertise."

For the author the story was about pride, the sin of sins. The pride of someone who wants to rescue someone else—"a therapeutic triumph," as we hear it called in clinics. Who dares question the wish for such an achievement? Is it not all we've got—one person trying to "help" another person, through the application of knowledge, understanding, intelligence? Infinite darkness before and after, but for a brief flicker of light, our one and only second here, a show of purpose, discovery, accomplishment. Is it an exaggeration or a distortion to connect such a defiant, Promethean hope with the work of a child psychologist, a reformatory social worker? Will it do to dismiss Sheppard as one of the lower breed, the naïve or relatively inadequate country bumpkin member of a profession which, in its higher realms, has had good cause to be proud—because, in fact, youths like the fourteen-year-old Rufus Johnson, the object of a clinician's insistence attention, have been reclaimed over and over again?

That word *reclaim*, kin to *rehabilitate*: one of my child psychiatrist supervisors, a first-rate psychoanalyst, used to use both words all the time. As we discussed the children I was learning to treat, she would talk about reclaiming or rehabilitating this one, of being destined to "lose" that one, no matter what we were to do. Those were heady, self-important, yet fatalistic days: the saved and the damned, the quick and the dead. Allen Wheelis, in a chapter entitled "The Vocational Hazards of Psychoanalysis" (at the end of *The Quest for Identity*) sums it all up—a temptation on the part of psychiatrists to regard themselves as gods. A banal temptation, these days: therapy as life for so many, one more instance of secular millennarianism. Here is Anna Freud, in her important book *Normality and Pathology in Childhood* (1969), writing what might be considered a brief social history of the American upper, educated bourgeoisie's experience with child rearing, and with much more—a spiritual crisis, a hunger that knew no filling:

> At the time when psychoanalysis laid great emphasis on the seductive influence of sharing the parents' bed and the traumatic consequence of witnessing parental intercourse, parents were warned against bodily intimacy with their children and against performing the sexual act in the presence of even their youngest infants. When it was proved in the analyses of adults that the withholding of sexual knowledge was responsible for many intellectual inhibitions, full sexual enlightenment at an early age was advocated. When hysterical symptoms, frigidity, impotence, etc., were traced back to prohibitions and the subsequent repressions of sex in childhood, psychoanalytic upbringing put on its program a lenient and permissive attitude toward the manifestations of infantile, pregenital sexuality. When the new instinct theory gave aggression the status of a basic drive, tolerance was extended also to the child's early and violent hostilities, his death wishes against parents and siblings, etc. When anxiety was recognized as playing a central part in symptom formation, every effort was made to lessen the children's fear of parental authority. When guilt was shown to correspond to the tension between the inner agencies, this was followed by the ban on all educational measures likely to produce a severe superego. When the new structural view of the personality placed the onus for maintaining an inner equilibrium on the ego, this was translated into the need to foster in the child the development of ego forces strong enough to hold their own against the pressure of the drives. Finally, in our time, when analytic investigations have turned to earliest events in the first year of life and highlighted their importance, these specific insights are being translated into new and in some respects revolutionary techniques of infant care.

She goes on to remark upon the hope, the faith, that was involved in all this: "In the unceasing search for pathogenic agents and preventive measures, it seemed always the latest analytic discovery which promised a better and more final solution of the problem." She acknowledges that some of the advice given to parents was useful; they were able to get on more easily and warmly with their children, who were, as well, spared various harsh or senseless practices. But there were disappointments. "Above all, to rid the child of anxiety proved an impossible task. Parents did their best to reduce the children's fear of them, merely to find that they were increasing guilt feelings, i.e., fears of the child's own conscience. Where in its turn, the severity of the superego was reduced, children produced the deepest of all anxieties, i.e., the fear of human beings who feel unprotected against the pressure of their drives."

Miss Freud tells us that the children who went through all that were, to be sure, different, but they were also human beings, and as such, subject to inevitable limitations: "It is true that the children who grew up under its influence were in some respects different from earlier generations; but they were not freer from anxiety or from conflicts, and therefore not less exposed to neurotic and other mental illnesses." She stresses, in further remarks, that "this need not have come as a surprise if optimism and enthusiasm for preventive work had not triumphed with some authors over the strict application of psychoanalytical tenets."

It is a contemporary kind of pride that Flannery O'Connor was interested in depicting—working into the grain of a few of her characters, among them, certainly, Sheppard. Perhaps Sheppard is drawn a bit implausibly. The author is writing a sardonic, tragic short story; she might have, even so, tried to explore the persistent, self-sacrificing idealism of this twentieth-century "shepherd." Instead, she takes a certain cast of mind for granted. In an authorial comment at the beginning of the story she observes that for Sheppard "almost any fault would have been preferable to selfishness—a violent temper, even a tendency to lie." We are given the irony that his own son, Norton, is behaving selfishly. We will soon enough learn that this boy, whose mother has died, is a terribly forlorn child, who needs desperately the kind of father his own father wants to be for a difficult, pugnacious delinquent. Norton commits suicide—the author's revenge, arguably, on "health care professionals" who go proselytizing everywhere (among people, often, who want no part of them) while neglecting to take care of their home fires. A not very original plot; a plot we all have conjured up in our minds at one time or another: the fire in the firehouse, the robbery in the police station, the unrecognized illness in the doctor's home.

But the author is after something more than an especially tasty irony. Her disinterest in the psychology of a psychologist is deliberate, and stubbornly maintained. She is stalking pride. She grabbed it from its everyday rural Georgia life and put it in story after story: collapsing southern pride; the pride of landowners, of preachers, of dirt-farmers, of mothers and sons and mothers and daughters and a grandfather and his grandson. Why not the pride of a "counselor," a reformer, "an agent of psychiatric change," as the dreary expression goes in what is called (speaking of ironies) "the literature?" It is a literature that Miss Anna Freud had very much in mind when she wrote the book mentioned above. A quite sensitive critic of Miss O'Connor, Miles Orvell, making a case for the implausibility of Sheppard, comments that "the point is not that such people (Sheppard) never have existed (they may, even as psychologists)—but as characters in a work of fiction, they fail to attain credibility." Needless to say, each reader will have to decide for himself or herself on that score. How does the portrait square with what obtains in real life? How suggestive and revealing are the author's points of ridicule, sarcasm, overstatement? Does the high coloring become false coloring—not a basis for vision, but a means to a dead end? Are we in the presence of indulgent extravagance or ill-informed rant?

No doubt a different writer, with a different sensibility, and as Miss O'Connor once put it, with "different fish to fry," could have taken the same, essential plot and evoked a poignance in Sheppard's life: the contours of human kindness—connected, as is often the case, with personal failings, or with the occurrence of tragedy. But this particular storyteller had a Christian's interest in pride, and her story is, really, one of pride in collision with pride in collision with pride. When a critic says "*even* as psychologists," and not with ironic intent, he is, also, telling us about a kind of pride: the professional pride that is so overwhelming that the judgment of an intelligent, sensitive, thoughtful reader is influenced. Rather than *even*, the word ought have been *especially*. Psychiatrists and psychologists are objects of faith—believed in by those for whom God is dead; "insight" or what it is supposed to bring, "emotional maturity," is all that is left. Arrogance, conniving, smugness, complacency, callousness—none of those attributes has failed to penetrate the mental skin of alienists, psychotherapists, psychiatric social workers, *et al*. Anyone who has been witness to the nasty gossip, the subtle and not so subtle put-downs, the insults or character insinuations that plague the various precincts of sectarian psychiatry (its cliques, schools, orientations, methodologies, approaches, and so on) would not be likely to deny this interesting twentieth-century social and cultural phenomenon the vulnerabilities Flannery O'Connor has chosen to underline—a blindness, an obtuseness, a weakness for bloated, self-serving language: the all too familiar instance of modern professionalism. To be sure, other professions are capable of producing such attitudes, ways of being and acting. Each of us is continually tempted by the sin of pride—or so the Bible tells us, and a Georgia writer recently wanted to say again. In a manner, it is the phrase "even as psychologists" that does indeed explain Miss O'Connor's intent: to expose the fierce self-centeredness that rules *even* those who claim to have analyzed out of themselves all sorts of conflicts, anxieties, phobias, "problems." As for the "credibility" of this figure Sheppard: is he any less credible than that nineteenth-century incarnation of monumental pride, Captain Ahab?

We are made uncomfortable, distressed, unnerved by the pious self-righteousness of a man who aims to be unstinting in his personal kindness to a stranger, a provocative, mean-spirited one, at that. Who is this Sheppard? What about him is so incredible? That he should compare his own son unfavorably, in certain respects, to a stranger—a troubled delinquent, no less? Is it so unlikely, really, that a certain kind of intensely humanitarian person could be so virtuously giving to the lowly, the base, even—and then turn on his own kin with annoyance or worse? We are given this comparison: "Johnson's sad thin hand rooted in garbage cans for food while his own child, selfish, unresponsive, greedy, had so much that he threw it up." Whereas the lame and belligerent Johnson "had a capacity for real response and had been deprived of everything from birth," the "counselor" Sheppard's son "was average or below and had had every advantage." Those words: *capacity, deprived, advantage*; they are the moral words of our time, the means by which all too many of us judge the worth of people. It is no longer a matter of each soul before God; it is no longer a matter of His inscrutable wisdom—or of the three Fates doing their mysterious work. The issues for us are psychological, sociological, but, as the author makes clear, the inclination toward moral judgment is not thereby diminished. As Sheppard put it: "Johnson's worth any amount of effort because he had potential." Another word: potential. Did Christ have it in mind, as He walked the roads of that outlying province of the Roman Empire and healed *His* lame, and promised *them* a boost toward a Heavenly rest? Did He go around evaluating "capacities" for this or that, and studying who was or was not psychologically capable of a "real response?" The author has such questions directly on her mind as she moves us right away from the above comparison a father makes between his son and his patient, to the following most interesting, and, I believe, utterly critical comparison, so far as the story goes, not to mention the teller's intentions: "Sheppard's office at the reformatory was a narrow closet with one window and a small table and two chairs in it. He had never been inside a confessional but he thought it must be the same kind of operation he had here, except that he explained, he did not absolve. His credentials were less dubious than a priest's; he had been trained for what he was doing."

Again, the words that go with professionalism: *credentials*, and *trained*—and the uses to which they are put. It is no matter-of-fact mental comparison this man has felt impelled to make. He is the smart one, the knowing one, and for us, in this culture, the chosen one. He is not here to forgive, but to "evaluate." And so he does, as precisely as he knows how. The next paragraph delivers a crushing reminder of what such a mentality relies upon—ideologically, rather than, sure enough, spiritually: "When Johnson came in for his interview, he had been reading over the boy's record—senseless destruction, windows smashed, city trash boxes set afire, tires slashed—the kind of thing he found where boys had been transplanted abruptly from the country to the city as this one had. He came to Johnson's I.Q. score. It was 140. He raised his eyes eagerly."

In one paragraph, and with no polemical gesture, the author has given us a glimpse of our unselfconscious sociological cast of mind: a move to the city as an "explanation" of crimes, if not sins. And then the pride: a bright patient! A mirror of himself, the therapist! And then the I.Q. score—the moral judgment of a number! A meritocratic version of Heaven and Hell. A Calvinism of quotients. And soon enough, the rally of interpretations, explanations, justifications. The boy had "a monstrous club foot." It was bound "in a heavy black battered shoe with a sole four or five inches thick." What to make of that? Everything: "The case was clear to Sheppard instantly." The boy's "mischief was compensation for the foot."

Is the author straining the plausible, the credible, the realistic with such a line of narration? The issue here is pride; and the other person's pride, Miss O'Connor knew, is always easier to accept, talk about, write about, than one's own. Arrogant businessmen are everywhere in evidence to liberal or radical academics, say—who easily dismiss any charge that they might have their own arrogant language or habits. And vice-versa. Miss O'Connor makes sure we know that the pride of the delinquent is as "monstrous" as that of his therapist. "The line of his thin mouth was set with pride," we are told—a youth standing fast against the attempted inroads of a man whose assumptions are regarded as altogether different. This is an "adolescent" who yells "Satan"; who insists that Satan has him "in his power." The author describes the "socio-cultural background," as social scientists put it, from which such belief has emerged: "This boy's questions about life had been answered by signs nailed on the pine trees: DOES SATAN HAVE YOU IN HIS POWER? REPENT OR BURN IN HELL. JESUS SAVES. He would know the Bible with or without reading it." The counselor has recognized an adversary—southern, rural, religious life. So doing, he falls back on his own ideas and ideals: "Where there was intelligence anything was possible." The kind of rumination soon gets put into the preliminary foray of a battle between two minds, and by extension, two cultures: "I'm going to arrange for you to have a conference with me once a week," the counselor tells his about-to-be patient. And adds: "Maybe there's an explanation for your explanation. Maybe I can explain your devil to you."

Miss O'Connor carefully develops the tension between the psychological mind of one person and the crime-driven, religion-haunted mind of another. It is interesting that critics worry about the construction of the counselor's character—as if the plausibility of the delinquent, Johnson, is of no real matter: another one of those southern freaks for which an author had a penchant. Yet, the portrayal of this youth, at once tough and hurt, resourceful and perversely stiff-necked, is strangely successful. Miss O'Connor demonstrates a brilliant sense of the canniness a certain kind of troubled youth can muster—a match, rather often, for even the best "trained" of us, who think of ourselves as graced by radarlike intelligence, able to pick up every single message sent our way. And she is altogether successful with the mind of this "therapist." In her own fashion she has conjured up the temptations that all the time threaten intellectuals—the treacherous self-satisfaction that spells spiritual doom.

The delinquent himself begins to realize how vain this apparently altruistic rescuer is. But the author doesn't throw such a development at us; she moves slowly toward it, a remarkably keen and patient build-up. If Miss O'Connor had no use for the present-day resort to psychology and psychotherapy as pagan religions, she held her grudge tightly in check:

> He had talked to Johnson every Saturday for the rest of the year. He talked at random, the kind of talk the boy would never have heard before. He talked a little above him to give him something to reach for. He roamed from simple psychology and the dodges of the human mind to astronomy and the space capsules that were whirling around the earth faster than the speed of sound and would soon encircle the stars. Instinctively he concentrated on the stars. He wanted to give the boy something to reach for besides his neighbor's goods. He wanted to stretch his horizons. He wanted him to *see* the universe, to see that the darkest parts of it could be penetrated. He would have given anything to be able to put a telescope in Johnson's hands.

The youth's pride persists. He doesn't yield, but his therapist begins to believe that he is "hitting dead center." The boy uses his clubfoot as a weapon and a shield: stay away, or else. The therapist fights on—calmly, persistently, ingeniously, intelligently, or so he hopes. He wants to channel energies misspent into what we all would regard as "constructive" directions. He understands his patient. He knows him—the terrible past, the fearful present, the anxiety about tomorrow, never mind next week, next year. And he begins to love him: fantasies of taking him in, working things out with him "in the home setting"—another expression of the clinic that blends that mixture of distance and intimacy which Miss O'Connor, in fact, is struggling hard to maintain between these two, at least in the early moments of their "relationship." And that is what she is sketching out, knowingly and tactfully. If we begin to squirm, it is because one of the two parties refuses to go along—ever. It is because we are witnessing the failure of what those in the so-called "helping professions" call an "approach." The more disarmingly "supportive" the therapist tries to be, the more reassuring he is, the more contemptuous the youth becomes. He is, indeed, what he has declared himself to be, a devilishly conniving character. He insinuates himself into his therapist's mind, then life—and the proudly "aware" therapist doesn't realize what is going on. A helper is trying to help someone who wants no such thing, but the harder the older one tries, the more elusive the younger one turns out to be.

For a while there is a standstill. The therapist persists in wanting to take the youth into his home—an ultimate escalation of "treatment" not unheard of: special circumstances require heroic efforts at retrieval. Delinquents especially stimulate in ardent therapists a Rousseau-like dream: this victim of so much worldly evil can yet be saved from his developing and severe "problems." But the youth (whose nasty talk and brutish behavior are viewed, with as much neutrality and equanimity as the counselor can mobilize, as "defensive mechanisms") won't take the "appropriate" steps, won't turn "constructive." At one point, after a good long time of acquaintance, the counselor makes a short speech. He is telling his son and his patient (and himself) why this exceedingly antisocial youth is to come live in the Sheppard household. Among the observations he offers, this one stands out: "I'd simply be selfish if I let what Rufus thinks of me interfere with what I can do for Rufus. If I can help a person, all I want is to do it. I'm above and beyond simple pettiness."

This is no oracular nonsense, the stuff of a writer intent on parody. It is a comment that snaps with the everyday reality of countless psychiatric clinics. I recall only too well the struggle waged in one of them to capture the right vocabulary, the right facial expression, the right tone of voice, the right manner of self-presentation. The self-assurance that risks turning into a needling haughtiness, a provocative presumptuousness. When Rufus Johnson tells the counselor Sheppard's son, Norton, that his father thinks he's Jesus Christ, we are not in the midst of a badly overwrought story, with an implausibility of character definition. We are distressingly close to a significant segment of this century's professional life.

I never read or use in class "The Lame Shall Enter First" without recalling a young delinquent I happened to work with myself as a "trainee" at a child psychiatry center in Boston, a part of the Children's Hospital. The young man had been remanded to us for treatment. He was not Rufus Johnson's fourteen, but eleven, a year older than Norton. This slight blond boy had set a string of fires, one of which had caused two deaths. He was, to be blunt, a child arsonist and murderer; and he looked like a choirboy in the nearest suburban Episcopal Church. As I talked with him, I remember thinking of Rousseau—the *tabula rasa* that had been (so early, so awfully) defaced. I remember wondering, too: *if*—the ifs of liberal agnosticism. The ifs that amount to a story: a boy is not born to be a murderer, an arsonist; it took years of incidents, experiences—meanness, brutality, psychological betrayal—to produce such an outcome. If he hadn't had an alcoholic, abusive father; if his mother hadn't been a seductive whore; if someone had spotted the psychopathology and done something, tried to mobilize "preventive measures" (in the clutch, legal ones) to remove the child from an extremely "abusive" family: *if*.

I recall the effort to "treat," to reach out, listen, watch, wait for words; to talk, if necessary—but we always hoped "they" (the patients) would do that, keep doing that, thereby enabling us to get a "history," to learn all the "psychodynamics," to "effect a change." We got lectures on such subjects: how to "effect psychological change." We noted with some pleasure our developing self-confidence as we began to notice, with patient after patient, that things were indeed happening. Of course when we said that such a development was taking place, we meant that it was all for the "good": a "positive transference," a "working relationship," evidence of an "involvement" on the part of yet another needy patient. But when things weren't going well, we were apt to turn on that poor patient with all we had: the "primitive" nature of his or her "defenses," the extremely "disturbed" quality of "early relationships," and on and on.

An outsider might have called us cross, frustrated, hurt at our inability to achieve something badly wanted—another's trust. We used longer words, the cumulative effect of which was to lean hard on those others we were treating. Certainly, there were nods to our own feelings, to the way we were inclined to deal with the "transference problems" of our patients. But the issue, of course, was the nature of those problems—distorted reactions to us, all based on early childhood experiences. Much less mention of *our* early childhood experiences—even as the psychoanalytic literature is heavily balanced in favor of a discussion of the way patients manipulate the "treatment relationship," as opposed to the manner in which their therapists might do likewise. And no mention at all given to any substantive objections that may have come up—a child's objection to the whole scene. One child did so, the boy just mentioned; he used those very words. I had just started my second year of a child psychiatry residency. I was surprised, saddened. He called us all in that clinic, all who came to "evaluate" him, members of a "whole scene," and he spelled out our membership tersely: "You're a bunch of ministers, trying to make everyone think like you do. Nothing doing. Not for me; nothing doing. Go back to your church!"

When I asked him *what* church, he refused to answer me. I thought I wanted his answer because thereby I'd learn more of what he feared in us, the doctors and psychologists and psychiatric social workers he'd so forcefully and rudely rebuffed. When he volunteered no amplification of his caustic remark, which in Flannery O'Connor's words, had ended up "hitting dead center," I had to decide that he was simply "striking out," more or less as Rufus Johnson did in "The Lame Shall Enter First." And my supervisor was more than helpful; he kept reminding me that delinquents are "tough" to treat, that they are extremely "aggressive interpersonally" as well as with respect to automobile locks or store doors, not to mention the faces and bodies of particular individuals. As for the remark about the church, I was reassured thoroughly: "He's probably heard a lot of religious talk when he was young."

Now such an apparently offhand observation was actually a rather complicated code message to me: this boy who is in possession, we had decided, of a "sociopathic personality" was not able to distinguish with any depth of conviction, with any sincerity, between right and wrong. He had, no doubt, been shouted at, hit furiously. But not out of an affectionate interest in teaching what ought be done, what mustn't be done. Rather, he'd been shouted down, made a scapegoat for sick, sick, sick adults. And maybe they were also religious: "Lots of people scream Jesus at others, and they're about three years old emotionally, even if they have grown up bodies, and they're parents." I remember nodding. No great surprise of a remark in the course of a psychiatric resident's educational voyage. But the ferocity of his injunction ("Go back to your church") had left its mark on me. I'd just read Allen Wheelis' discussion, mentioned above—his description of the god-like stance many of us in my profession take with respect to our patients, *and* ourselves: our sense of who we are, and what the significance is of our every spoken word.

Miss O'Connor splits her story in half, ends the first part with that sharp judgment, that brilliant insight: Sheppard as, in his own estimate, the Son of God. The rest of the story is a judgment of another kind: the traditional tragedy that befalls hubris. A man has shaken his fist at the heavens, shown he dares dismiss another's faith, however flawed its human vessel—and even shown a wish to turn someone else into a copy of himself. The response of the avenging heavens is swift, terrible. The Bible-talking delinquent comes into the home of the psychology-thinking counselor, whose motherless son becomes, in no time, a pawn of retribution. Deftly, shrewdly, the author moves her light from one to another shadowy element in the relationship of these three: the delinquent's wayward brilliance—a powerful, if malevolent defense against smug, opinionated knowledge; the counselor's self-centeredness, fanatically summoned in the apparent service of another's salvation, but increasingly revealed as its own unyielding master; and a child's lost, fragile, anxious soul—used by one person, ignored by another, claimed at last by (we are given to believe) a desperately sought God.

An intellectual storyteller is taking pains to separate God's kingdom from man's, the saved from the damned, the just from the unjust. But she shuns neat psychological categories. Finally, we are judged elsewhere than on earth. Her task as a novelist is to let each character shed light on how life is variously lived. The delinquent acts, sins, quotes from the Bible. The child reveals the pride that innocence only masks—the Original Sin that we who describe early childhood reject as an explanation for the assertiveness, the petulance, the spitefulness, the egoism to be found in boys and girls. (As for the "aggression," the "oedipal rivalry" and jealousy and hostility we feel more comfortable describing, they are treatable.) The counselor takes on the entire universe. He buys a telescope for his charge, then a microscope: "If he couldn't impress the boy with immensity, he would try the infinitesimal." He is unceasingly the reformer, the man who will turn around the seeming destiny of another. A troubled mind will be heard, rendered whole through patient understanding. A lame leg will also be attended—a new, right-fitting shoe.

But the boy refuses to talk about what any therapist would call his problems; he also refuses the orthopedic rehabilitation extended him. His counselor thinks him "not mature enough" to want to wear the new shoe. What to do but wait and hope? The author has Sheppard "glumly entrenched behind the Sunday New York *Times*." Maybe an unnecessary touch, but hardly an inappropriate symbol. Miss O'Connor knows that, in the clutch, we all fall back on what we have—in this case, a Sunday paper that for the Sheppards of this land stands for moderation, rationality, a cosmopolitan outlook. Language also serves to reassure us—words such as *insecurity*, the *self* and of course, *identity*.

The harder Sheppard clings to his particular faith, the nearer he brings himself and his young patient to the edge of things. The youth is full of outrage, won't yield an inch of his self. He regards Sheppard as, ironically, a fraud: a would-be Christ, therefore the greatest sinner of all. In contrast he, Johnson (or is it John the Baptist's Son?) believes in Christ, believes the Devil has claimed him from Christ, believes no one can save him "but Jesus." Another one of Miss O'Connor's, and our heretics—a Jansenist dressed up as a clubfooted delinquent? Yes or no, some will argue that this engagement or confrontation is staged, all too calculated. How "real" is Sheppard?

Sheppard is, if anything, a character whose moral flaws are understated. His vanity emerges gradually—is suggested discreetly. He is not blind to his shortcomings. He is caught in a cultural web he never thought to examine—so busy was he examining the heads of others.

We are not asked, in the tradition of Nietzsche, to embrace this raging, animal-like young man as the repository of nature's (antiacademic) truth. There is nothing heroic about the delinquent youth, Johnson. This is one of Flannery O'Connor's harshest, most vexing stories, especially difficult for her readers to take, precisely because the soft psychological and moral belly of secular, agnostic liberalism is not exposed by a saint, or a marvelous religious polemicist in the Dostoievsky tradition. Filling in for Alyosha, and Ivan, too, is a dreary wise guy, a bully who deserves to be locked up for a good long time. But a bully with a working knowledge of the Bible. A bully who knows he's going to hell—and who has a sharp eye out for others, who may well already be there! An irony of ironies in this story, is the eventual realization, too late, by the counselor of *his* mental dodges, the evasions he uses, which put others in their places, so to speak, but leave him homeless.

"Satan has you in his power," Johnson tells Sheppard; then the youth stresses, "Not only me. You too." No self-righteousness from a disciple of Satan; rather, a candid claim that there are a lot more fellow travelers than someone may realize. Meanwhile, the counselor plays his last card, scoffs at the Bible, pulls out one interpretation after another from the psychological canon he has mastered, and slides into the despair he has avoided only by concentrating with all his mind and heart upon another's condition. Miss O'Connor does not, of course, object to such a devotion; nor is she working up a propaganda tract for Satan. She isn't really "against" psychology or psychiatry in the conventional, ideological sense of that preposition, "against." She is trying to dramatize an incompatibility she has seen about her in this modern world: intellectuals who mock traditional religion, then take a certain religious way of getting along with others; and believers of the Word, of the Book, who are challenged these days in a new manner, and who must defend themselves, as has been the case over the centuries, with every bit of guile it is possible to summon.

The suicide of Norton is no mere melodramatic ending, by a writer unafraid of violence. The boy dies with his own willful faith intact. He has launched a flight into space. He told his father that through the telescope he saw his (dead) mother—up there, waving to him. The father had, once more, interpreted "reality," made his clarification, taken on an illusion, without coming to terms with his own illusion—that, thereby, he is addressing himself to the mysteries and confusions of this terrible life so many of us live, his son included. We are left in the end, ironically, with psychology: a father who has neglected his own son in favor of a troubled patient, ends up losing both, the one to the police and the other in consequence of a suicide. But another point of view would insist that we are left with something else. Many times on the side of rural Georgia roads such as those the delinquent youth in this harsh and sad story could well have traveled, I have seen a cautionary sign that may well serve as a summation of the author's implicit moral lesson: PRIDE KILLETH.

The intellectual's version of pride is something Flannery O'Connor knew in herself. Her letters are exceptional in their lack of self-centeredness. She had no big ego, waiting for a vulnerable correspondent. She mocked her own work. She loved to write in plain, southern country vernacular: no airs, ever. She looked deep into herself. Tactful, polite, able to laugh at anyone's pretensions, including a few quiet ones of her own, she was not inclined to settle for less than a thorough skepticism that included all humanity: even her fellow Catholics, even herself, as well as those she often took to task for their agnosticism or rootless sophistication. "Smugness is the Great Catholic Sin," she told one of her correspondents. Then, this: "I find it in myself and don't dislike it any less." She could also acknowledge her "ego"; and she once said: "So I wait for purgatory." But she wasn't excessively self-critical—a clever kind of pride. She knew where her soul was weak; she mentioned once that her upbringing had smacked a little of Jansenism. Not her convictions, she added; her stories, by indirection, refute Jansenism. Like the rest of us, however, she felt the tension between those two great mental forces in this life—what we learned to feel and think as boys and girls, and what we came to think as we set out on our own, grown-up journey. Her letters show the influence of the Augustinian tradition, despite her affinity for Thomistic rationalism. She saw and wrote of that tension—between the reasonable side of human beings and the constant temptation toward flights of fancy, with the attendant risk of self-indulgence.

Her portraits of Hulga, of Julian, of Asbury, three intellectuals of sorts, are affecting if also comic, and, at moments, harshly sardonic.

Without question these are tough stories to read for any small-town, or even big-city southern man or woman who has fought his or her way out of certain cultural constraints. Hulga, in "Good Country People," may, in the end, reveal *her* smugness, her Jansenist inability to connect her brain's life to the surrounding life of a southern rural scene. But she is also, quite clearly, a decent visionary, who can't stand the crudities and stupid pieties that pass for daily talk in her mother's home. Miss O'Connor is prepared, throughout this extremely funny story, to let the blind lead the blind—or maybe, finish one another off. The following parody of intellectual reading (and of our twentieth-century attachment to logical positivism) is offered as a quote from a book of Hulga's, opened by her prying mother, Mrs. Hopewell: "Science, on the other hand, has to assert its soberness and seriousness afresh and declare that it is concerned solely with what is. Nothing—how can it be for science anything but a horror and a phantasm? If science is right, then one thing stands firm: science wishes to know nothing of nothing. Such is after all the strictly scientific approach to Nothing. We know it by wishing to know nothing of Nothing." That was underlined, we are told—by an author pushing us hard to think of the dreary junk that ends up as impressive to "the girl [who] had taken the Ph.D. in philosophy." But the foolish optimism of Mrs. Hopewell (another O'Connor name meant to match a character's point of view) is no more appealing. And her daughter can be attractively blunt and down-to-earth—her cynicism a balance to the mother's fatuousness.

In the end, knowledge is no match for the workings of pride, a familiar O'Connor theme. Mother and daughter alike are taken in by a crafty Bible salesman whose triumph is not, however, achieved through his own abilities as a confidence man. It is the sadness, the loneliness, of a mother, a daughter, that sets them both up for various assaults. The author knows how quickly her readers will dismiss Mrs. Hopewell, and take an instinctive interest in the dour, shrewdly observant Mrs. Freeman—who may well be the person meant to exemplify a certain kind of intellectuality: coldly attentive to all that is wrong in the world; pessimistic, if not sour and crabbed; willing, always, to feast off the failures, the disasters, the accidents, and tragedies of the world. Mrs. Freeman will be taken in by no one. Mrs. Hopewell and her daughter are, in different respects, Mrs. Freeman's prey. The salesman is a brief version of the longer-lasting Mrs. Freeman: the darkness of the world, ever present. Though some readers emphasize the harsh treatment given Hulga, and through her, Mrs. Hopewell, the author can as well be showing us how difficult it is for such relatively decent people to survive—even in that very "country" part of the South mentioned with such affection at times in *The Habit of Being*, and *Mystery and Manners*.

In "Good Country People," an author's anti-intellectualism is given controlled rein. She spoofs Hulga's braininess, shows it wanting in a struggle with a devilishly intuitive country salesman, but in the end makes clear her conviction that there are worse ones around than the Hulgas of the world. She has flirted with nihilism, with the Devil. Her visitor *is* the Devil: "And I'll tell you another thing, Hulga, you ain't so smart. I been believing in nothing ever since I was born!" Before we come to that final moment of ironic circularity, we experience its predecessor—Hulga's wrong-headed condescension. O'Connor spoofs Kierkegaard's concept of the "teleological suspension of the ethical" —Abraham's surrender of his son Isaac to God, in the full knowledge that He may take the son's life. Hulga realizes at one point that "for the first time in her life she was face to face with real innocence." The boy wanted to see her artificial leg. She refused him. He persisted. She asked him why. He got to her with: "It's what makes you different. You ain't like anybody else." Pride of a certain kind. When he told her of her uniqueness she became his. "All right," she says; and the author has her thinking to herself that "it was like surrendering to him completely," and further, "it was like losing her own life and finding it again, miraculously in his." A kind of resignation. A kind of religious experience—a parodic version of what we are told in the New Testament happens when one finds Christ. An intellectual's conversion, and as such, a false turn because it was not made with all her heart and mind and soul.

I saw other signs along those good country roads of rural Georgia: PRIDE KILLETH, as mentioned earlier; but also, PRIDE DECEIVETH. Satan is always waiting along such roads, ready to take what we as exiles from the Garden are prepared (by virtue of our lack of *proper* preparation) to give him. In this story of pride, an intellectual's pity becomes an instrument of her seduction, her psychological unmasking. The contempt she has had for others, the lower orders, soon enough turns into the rage of a person undone by an action of misplaced trust. Nor is brainy hauteur any match for a serpentine canniness that operates without the slightest tortuosity of thought. "Flattery will get you nowhere" is the kind of silly remark a girl pining for attention makes to her suitor—an invitation masked as a refusal. How the self-styled mighty fall victim to the oldest and most humdrum of ploys, enacted in thousands and thousands of automobiles, after untold numbers of high school proms! Doctoral candidates, doctors of philosophy, ought know better, a Mrs. Hopewell might say. Mrs. Freeman would, alas, know better; and it is she who gets the last word in "Good Country People."

Miss O'Connor's treatment of Julian and Asbury, the two somewhat aimless and weak southern liberal young men, is also connected to her complicated attitude toward intellectuals, many of whose ideas she shared. What she doesn't like about both those men is a certain snobbishness they can't help demonstrating—a wry insouciance toward the feelings of their own kin, and in contrast, a complete devotion to the values and feelings of certain others: the distant liberals of Yankeedom, the nearby blacks, or the South's own progressive people. Several critics have insisted that none of O'Connor's characters beg the reader's "identification," but I wonder whether there aren't a few of us liberals, southern or northern, who haven't found in ideas, in political argument, and alas, in the impatience we feel toward our old friends and members of our own family, a source of the very smug ness Flannery O'Connor worried about in herself.

Julian and Asbury not only *have* those (liberal, progressive, and in the context of a time, a place, radical) ideas; the two discreet rebels *use* those ideas in various confrontations with their mothers, and really, with the black and white people they come into contact with. We've worked over "Everything That Rises Must Converge" fairly thoroughly in that regard. "The Enduring Chill" has the twist of a southerner gone North, then compelled to come home, sick—and soon enough, we discover, sickened by what he sees and hears: the backwoods mentality of the rural South. But we become sickened with him—the author's intention, surely. Even the local and loyal blacks, whom he dramatically wants to favor (and become personally integrated with, in a manner of speaking) end up confused, impatient, anxious to be back in their own, familiar world, segregated by race and class, rather than in the contrived presence of this ever so thoughtful, sensitive man—who, nevertheless, is standing up for all the "right" things. Liberal humanism, yet again, gets a tough, sometimes scathing going over. Yet, we're not happy with the ignorant attitudes of Timberboro—*its* smugness, narrowness, and one has to say it, the racism that is part of the life depicted there. It is important to realize that Miss O'Connor does do that depicting. Lest the sarcasm she pours upon the liberal-intellectual Asbury be allowed to overwhelm the reader, she can stop everything, including, maybe, her own satirical intentions, with this observation: "He had been writing a play about Negroes (why anybody would want to write a play about Negroes was beyond her) and he had said he wanted to work in the dairy with them and find out what their interests were."

At this point we are ready to conclude that an esthete who won't end up writing any play at all is in a conflict with a bigot with social airs—hardly one to earn our sympathies. And when the author tells us, acidly, that "their [the Negroes'] interests were in doing as little as they could get by with, as she could have told him if anybody could have told him anything," we are not ready to gloat over this triumph of a maternal sensibility. Nor are we pleased when the authorial voice reminds us that blacks are made nervous by the likes of an Asbury. In her own indirect way, the author presents a devastating picture of segregationist swagger and intimidation—fought weakly, perhaps, and out of vanity, no doubt, and with a killing intellectual pride; but nevertheless fought. Haven't we the right to say, in retrospect, that in the 1950s, when this story was written, such an idiosyncratic, feeble white resistance to segregation was about all that there was to see in the small-town and rural South? And such resistance, Miss O'Connor makes clear, was quite often the intellectual's. A tortured stand. An inherently futile one, perhaps—no money, no clout. But a stand the author chooses not to ignore, and not *only* to satirize.

Miss O'Connor's treatment of the somewhat intellectual figure Rayber in her second novel *The Violent Bear It Away* presents rather a different issue. The novel was a hard one for her to write. Several times in *The Habit of Being* she remarks upon her troubles with the plot, and especially with the character Rayber. She knew the dangers of her own pride, her own prejudices. She could say, as mentioned earlier, that she had "a stomach full of liberal religion!"; she could also refer to "all the stupid Yankee liberals" (1963). Why not caricature them through Rayber? And to be sure, some critics are convinced that she did just that. We are told by a friend of hers that the author knew, after the novel had been finished, that she failed to do a good job with Rayber, make him something more than a liberal agnostic, all caught up with psychology and a few "humanistic perspectives," the title, these days, of courses in southern as well as Yankee colleges. I doubt she ever would have, could have, portrayed a godless intellectual in such a way that he or she triumphs over a person of the spirit, no matter how strange and apparently idiosyncratic that spirit happened to be. But I don't think she has been given enough credit for Rayber—who isn't the main character of the novel, in any case. Certainly there are moments when satire gets overworked. I wish Miss O'Connor hadn't equipped him with a hearing aid. I also thought she worked a little too hard with Tarwater, who doesn't exactly come across as clean, pure, and holy.

Obviously the author wants us to consider Tarwater and Rayber together—and, in a way, makes the outcome of the novel the result of their strong, tense, almost violent encounter. Tarwater's great uncle had wanted him to take up the mission of biblical prophesy: bury the old man; baptize an idiot cousin, Bishop, living with his father, Rayber, in the city; walk forward into the world as one of God's faithful preachers. The nephew Tarwater resists, yet is also carried along. He goes to see Rayber and Bishop, and a good part of the novel has to do with their carryings-on: a man moving to accept but also fighting the prophesy that he ought and will preach the Holy Word meets a teacher all full of the tenets of educational psychology. It is not an unfamiliar O'Connor confrontation. Put differently, it is a battle between faith as embodied in the old-time, evangelical Christian tradition and secular modernity, with its strong intellectual bulwark: physics, experimental neurophysiology, the social sciences—a thoroughly materialist viewpoint.

Caricature is applied on both sides; the author is, one can't repeat too often, a humorist, among other things. She loves action in the service of a laugh. She also gives us liquor, a big fire, plenty of ranting and raving, a drowning, a deftly handled and very funny roadside seduction scene. And she gives us those highways, leading to and from the city, with strangers ready to pick up strangers—the loneliness and hunger for talk, for someone to listen. Christ the onetime wayfarer—and all of today's interstates, full of people on the go, on the go. Where to, and with what purpose? Rayber wants mental health, a well-adjusted personality—and a whole bunch of I.Q. points for his idiot son. Rayber wants an end to superstition. He wants teachers who have an eye out for "emotions." He wants visual aids; he wants audiovisual aids; he wants everyone to see through everything—the sham, the hocus-pocus, of the benighted and those who play on their fears, trick them: best described as conjurers rather than prophets.

Still, these two men are not only emblematic figures in an author's personal and artistic struggle to make us, through her fiction, witnesses to a given century's version of the continuing struggle between those who recognize and fear God and those who have turned their backs on Him in favor of themselves. Both men, after all, are of the same biblical stock. Both are descendants of a prophet, and each is strong-willed, capable of frenzy, guile, and, not least, despair, which is a version of pride. (We give up because we have less faith in God's purposes than in our own sense of what matters.) Neither man is without complexity, ambiguity. Tarwater doesn't only seek out Rayber to win over his pitiable son for Christ. Tarwater is not only driven by his "wise blood" but by a desire to test his ideas, come to terms with them by coming to terms with someone who defines them through opposition. Rayber is, naturally, the logical choice—wise blood as against bad blood. The intellectual as the Devil. And so they meet, and come to grips, and through their exchanges provide the reader with yet another sharply worded, though comic, debate: Faith as against Reason. Faith at all costs, Faith blindly stated, against Reason not always undercut with sarcasm.

The reader can't help remembering, every once in a while, that the Tarwaters of this world don't write novels; the Raybers wish they could, but lack the inspiration. It is a mixture of the two that many of us hope for, a Faith that doesn't allow the Intellect to become a victim of Pride. I am not so sure that Miss O'Connor dares tell us exactly what a right-thinking prophet has in his mind or soul as he goes about his earthly journey. Paul's injunction is a hard one to spell out in prescriptive detail: "not of the letter, but of the spirit: for the letter killeth, but spirit giveth life." Tarwater is pulled by doubt as well as a growing conviction that there are ordained (better, fore-ordained) tasks for him to accomplish. Rayber is tormented by the disappointments life has sent his way: a son whose brain won't work right, being thereby a living mockery of what seems all-important to secular man—his own head. These are not two neatly stereotypic foils for an author's prejudices.

One of the best scenes in O'Connor's fiction is Rayber's pursuit of Tarwater, who ends up inside an evangelical "temple," where a child evangelist is preaching a fiery fundamentalist sermon. Her message prompts a brief but powerful clash of faiths: the liberal humanist, who worries about hurt and suffering children, everywhere exploited by ignorance, poverty, the manipulations of their craven elders, as against the Christian, who knows that suffering is, inevitably, what life is about—suffering and mystery. Even before the child begins her passionate sermon, Rayber is more tempted by her than he has any way of knowing: "It was the thought of a child's mind warped, of a child led away from reality that always enraged him." A girl holding her arms up high, exhorting a crowd with high-pitched intensity and considerable brilliance becomes for him—he is outside, peering through the window—a reminder of what he himself might have become.

The girl's message is brilliantly rendered. Miss O'Connor knows not to patronize southern child evangelists. I've heard a number of them, and the inspired accuracy of this version carried me back in time. "Oh, ye unbelievers," I once heard a girl of thirteen say right to me (and no one else, I was then quite certain) in an open-air meeting outside West Point, Mississippi: 1961, and all white. And she went on, lashing into the exalted sense of self that characterizes what she kept calling the "godless people." We can invent anything, she reminded us technocrats, think anything, she reminded us social scientists, but we "can't become what we aren't." A considerable pause. Surely, my wife and I thought, she won't spell *that* out! She'll pray for us, the lost ones. But she did: "You are all you've got—sinners leading sinners, the blind leading the blind. Yet you pray!" Another pause. A lapse of logic on her part? A mind hungry for such a lapse is ready to clap. Then she delivers her wallop: "You pray to yourselves. You are heathens in search of a god, and you always find one; you listen to your own words, and pray to yourselves for more and more of them."

A lot of words on *her* part, a "defensive" listener is quick to think. And then a version of Rayber the rescuer comes to life with *his* words: what is a *child* doing, coming up with all that talk? Does she go to school? A pawn in an unscrupulous parental confidence game—the child used to bring in the dough? Interpretations such as those, at once social and psychological, come rather easily to a certain kind of mind, as Flannery O'Connor well knew. But occasionally a preacher penetrates the mind that comes up with those interpretations. One realizes oneself in the presence of a spectacle—in St. Paul's words: "For I think that God hath set forth us the apostles last, as it were appointed to death: for we are made a spectacle unto the world, and to angels, and to men."

The puritanism in Southern Evangelicalism can suddenly disappear. A passion of exhortation reaches the listener, induces an excitement that is infectious, palpable, quite threatening to a skeptical, cerebral onlooker. No, one thinks. No, one insists. No, one concludes—after summoning, as in a war, everything one's got: who *are* these people, and why do they shout so, and why do those who listen end up shouting so, and what is the *reason* for such goings-on, and that child, that mere child, that hollering, crying, overexcited, terribly wrought-up child—what will happen to her, in the future, if *this* is her (determining) past? Only later does one remind oneself that these people have not divested themselves of clothes or calories or memories or sexual feelings, as others, elsewhere, do. These people, quite simply, became awestruck. Their silence on that Mississippi summer night was uncanny. The stars seemed noisier than anything alive below them. A mosquito going about its business suddenly reminded one listening victim of what had been interrupted—a lull that seemed endless. And suddenly, the human voice again: "Thank you for praying to Him, you sinners. I know some of you don't believe; but I heard your hush. You stopped listening to yourselves, even if you didn't start hearing Him talk, our one and only Lord, Jesus Christ."

A reverie—brought back to a mind while reading of Rayber, crouching on the ground, his hungry eyes excited almost uncontrollably by a child evangelist's presence. The author uses the word *transfixed* to describe what happened to Rayber for a moment or two. He was not won over, converted; nor, in the other direction, was he alarmed, horrified. He was tempted by her: "Rayber's heart began to race. He felt some miraculous communication between them. The child alone in the world was meant to understand him." A moment of weakness? A moment of hysterical identification with a crowd—or with the overwrought speaker? The listener may not have been brought to Christ, but he was brought to himself, or at least a hidden part of himself, as we learn when Rayber and Tarwater leave the tabernacle. For a few moments, Tarwater is approachable—is ready, almost, to turn his back on a prophetic calling, turn toward Rayber with a willingness to hear, pay heed, follow. The tough, defiant young man becomes strangely gentle; he wants to talk with Rayber, rather than provoke him. But he meets up with a suddenly different companion—not the friendly, talkative, willingly open Rayber, but a cold, shut-off man.

In an excellent article, the southern literary critic Louis D. Rubin, Jr., asks why the strange and pivotal transformation in both parties takes place: Rayber uninterested in Tarwater just at the moment when the latter has turned toward the former. Rubin's answer is helpful. Rayber had become taken with the child evangelist; the result was a reaction: "It is the schoolteacher's fear of the emotion of love that prevents him from being able to help Tarwater." The girl had almost, but not quite, broken through his shell of rationalism, intellectualism. As soon as he and Tarwater left her and her spellbound listeners, Rayber had to protect his newly vulnerable self in the face of Tarwater's newly conciliatory approaches.

I would only make a slight addition. Miss O'Connor nowhere does better with intellectuals than here. Is it that the child evangelist has threatened a person's defenses, and so prompted a tightening up in him, at just the point that he seems within grasp of what he has eagerly sought—*his* conversion of a young man's soul to the materialism of behavior psychology? Or is it that a shrewd novelist has moved us toward a *revelation*? Every evangelist I've heard has used that last word —often upon quoting from the gripping last book of the New Testament, the Revelation of St. John the Divine. Here was the ultimate in a Savior's prophesy, mediated by one of His followers. Here was everything an old Tarwater could want for a younger version of himself: an unyielding distinction spelled out—a future apocalypse, whereupon the saved and the damned will go their separate ways. And what southern revival religion wants in general, Rayber got: a revelation, a final statement of what is meant to be. Rayber has had a dream of conquest, and seen it slip through his fingers. For a few seconds the girl had become an object of his passionate interest; *he* would save *her*. But she turned from him, on him; denounced him. Spurned, angered, his self-centeredness wounded, he pulls into himself. A preacher's vanity exposed by another preacher. He not only feared that he would be undone enough to reveal his emotional side; he was a disappointed, beaten man who revealed the behaviorist's cult of self that is mechanistic, coldly calculating, psychologically reductionist. The apparent Rayber (an inviting rationalist who wants to explain, clarify, offer the interpreter's handshake) gives way to the "real" Rayber; the prideful intellectual who, thwarted or crossed or let down, shows himself to be decisively cold, overbearing, and (emotionally) "violent." So it will go one day, when the quick and the dead get sorted out.

It may be that the above moment in her second novel turned out to be Flannery O'Connor's harshest judgment on our century's intellectuals. She caricatured them in her stories; she condemned them in her essays; she gave them the back of her hand, repeatedly, in her letters. But in this particular scene of her painfully wrought novel (seven years in the making) she places intellectuals symbolically in Hell—cold, cold people, unable to respond to others on any terms but their own: the pedant in search of a willing admirer. The child evangelist, Tarwater, young Bishop—all are the same: objects to be regarded with calculating, clinical circumspection by a man whose heart is a stone.

Not that Tarwater is recommended as an alternative. This is no book about personality, the mature kind and the immature kind. This is no either/or story; nor is it a duel that is won or lost, pure and simple, by A or by B. Bishop is baptized—but killed; Tarwater will pursue a Bible-haunted life. The author relentlessly documents the continuing violence that bears away our world—the decency in people a loser time and again to various schemers, not the least of which are those who talk a good game about reform: social scientists of various kinds, with their endless plans meant to banish all the woes the world has ever known. But in the name of such ambitious virtuosity there crawl dozens of serpents—prophets the match of old, demanding, relentless Tarwater; prophets smug and mannered and pretentious enough to make both the child evangelist and the younger Tarwater seem like pleasant innocents, like "fools for Christ."

Flannery O'Connor's intellectual life, rich and deep and complex and by her own choice decidedly restricted, is best approached with her regional roots in mind, as well as her strongly felt, binding religious commitment. She had no use for all the Confederate junk, physical and symbolic, that has continued to obsess certain southerners. She was not especially worked up over the race issue, pro or con; she saw Dr. King to be doing what he had to do—and in that regard, her resentment at those who wanted to push her to say more "liberal" things was not a reaction of the segregationist standing fast in the last ditch. She had a sharp eye for the faddism in our intellectual life—an aspect, she knew, of a rootlessness others like her have described with the same regret, and sometimes, foreboding. Simone Weil, in *The Need for Roots*, gives us aphoristic remarks such as "uprootedness breeds idolatry," or with respect to the word *intellectuals*, the following description: "an awful name, but at present they scarcely deserve a better one." These two remarkably independent and gifted women, who shared eighteen years of time on this planet, had a similar religious sensibility—and a common willingness to see in exceptional brilliance dangers as well as opportunities.

For O'Connor, Weil was an obvious source of fascination and, at times, inspiration. She read that French rationalist (and, ultimately, religious mystic) with considerable attentiveness. She comments upon her at great length in her letters. Even more interesting, there are remarks that suggest not only a profound intellectual engagement but an artistic response that, alas, was never permitted by fate to materialize: "Simone Weil's life is the most comical life I have ever read about and the most truly tragic and terrible. If I were to live long enough and develop as an artist to the proper extent, I would like to write a comic novel about a woman—and what is more comic and terrible than the angular intellectual proud woman approaching God inch by inch with ground teeth?"

Lest we find in those words yet another snide put-down of an extremely significant life—in the interests of what gets called psychological realism or psychohistory, she has this to say: "By saying Simone Weil's life was both comic and terrible, I am not trying to reduce it, but mean to be paying her the highest tribute I can. short of calling her a saint, which I don't believe she was." Then, in clarification to the friend addressed: "Possibly I have a higher opinion of the comic and terrible than you do. To my way of thinking it includes her great courage and to call her anything less would be to see her as merely ordinary. She was certainly not ordinary. Of course, I can only say, as you point out, this is what I see, not, this is what she is—which only God knows."

The intellectual renunciation in that last observation was, no doubt, hard for a mind of such penetrating brilliance. Miss O'Connor knew that she required a bit more distance on herself, if she was really to understand Simone Weil, let alone write a novel about a life such as hers. She is exceptionally candid about her own life when she writes to a friend about Miss Weil, whom so many have described as saintlike. To the same correspondent O'Connor had been, off and on, sending comments about Simone Weil the following was offered: "My heroine already is, and is Hulga. Miss Weil's existence only parallels what I have in mind, and it strikes me especially hard because I had it in mind before I knew as much as I do now about Simone Weil. Hulga in this case would be a projection of myself into this kind of tragic-comic situation—presumably only a projection, because if I could not stop short of it myself, I could not write it. Stop short or go beyond it, I should say. You have to be able to dominate the existence that you characterize."

Those are reflections that come as close psychologically to what is called creativity as anyone in psychiatry has ever gotten, or is ever apt to get. They are at once autobiographical and philosophical. The writer uses restraint when she alludes to herself, yet indicates that she is willing to connect herself with one of her characters—provided she be permitted as much personal leeway in the matter as she would always insist for her characters. Put differently, the intellectual who worried about the risks that go with abstract attitudes—the way they can confine the minds of readers, cut off imaginative possibilities, cast shadows on one set of truths in the interest of emphasizing the presence of another aspect of reality—was not about to let herself be excluded from the caveats she had been uttering. She, too—any of us—is entitled to a little protection when someone's effort is required to make a psychological characterization.

She knew her own kind of pride and as a devout Catholic she no doubt waged a lifelong, prayerful struggle with herself—with her mind's self-importance, with a sinful yearning (pride) that goes back historically (or some would say, mythologically) to the Garden of Eden. Her wonderfully knowing response to Simone Weil, that most idiosyncratic of twentieth-century religious pilgrims, is perhaps confessional in nature. And the offhand, indeed parenthetical remark, "which only God knows," quoted above, reveals yet again the deeply felt nature of her suspicion about intellectual activity.

Even though Flannery O'Connor loved St. Thomas Aquinas, read him again and again, quoted from him; even though she took on the considerable if rewarding challenge of Pierre Teilhard de Chardin, whom she repeatedly mentions in her letters; even though she read and understood Jacques Maritain; her Catholic intellectualism remained precisely that—always *sub specie aeternitatis*. She knew the (sinful) dangers of confusing the use of an intelligence (God-given) with the resort to ideas as a last court of appeals, as a fundamental act of self-definition. She had no psychological inhibition with respect to the intellect; it was hers to develop, call upon, enjoy. But she had to keep in mind ownership, and yes, transcendence. For her, the intellect was a gift, and the Donor was Someone in particular—God become a man in history. For her the intellect was, thereby, a responsibility—something on loan, as it were. And for her, the intellect was, always, but one element in life, and by no means the essence of it. Even as she believed in a tripartite God, she believed as well in the tripartite nature of the human being—body, mind and soul.

The soul for her had its own life, its own requirements. Anyone who confused it with the mind, or tried to extend the word *soul*, was for her badly confused, if not wicked. In an interesting letter to her friend Cecil Dawkins (1962), she acknowledged "quite a respect for Freud when he isn't made into a philosopher." She was quite willing to put him alongside her beloved St. Thomas Aquinas: "They are rowing in the same boat." A high compliment, indeed, from her. "To religion," she added, "I think he [Freud] is much less dangerous than Jung." Jung, the man who had given the prestigious Terry lectures in religion at Yale (*Modern Man in Search of a Soul*), and who had written so much on the legitimacy of a need for religion, was far preferable to the man who had written *The Future of an Illusion!* Why? Flannery O'Connor, a Thomist, wasn't really interested in what Freud had to say about religion. He could still call it an illusion a million times, for all she cared. She knew that the illusion in question was *his*—the notion that psychological maneuvers "explain" what faith "means" or "is."

She also knew what people have done with Freud in this century—and not completely without his acquiescence. He acknowledged his own political fantasies, his identification with the military leader Hannibal. He was not only a doctor, a thinker, a writer; he became the leader of a worldwide *movement*, as it has been called all along. And he became, and for many still is, someone who has the answers for more than questions about the mind's everyday functional life. His ideas have become hardened into tablets of law. In the epilogue to *Childhood and Society*, Erik H. Erikson refers to "talmudic argument," "messianic zeal," and "punitive orthodoxy" as aspects of psychoanalytic life that must be looked at and admitted as distinctly possible dangers in the young psychiatrist's training experience, not to mention the nature of the older psychiatrist's teaching.

As for Jung, he was more dangerous, she realized, because he was attempting to meddle directly in religion. Freud, like everyone else, struggled with pride; and his followers, like many people, craved a godlike leader. But Jung felt he had an explicity religious answer; his psychological knowledge had taken him, never mind his cohorts, into the realms of philosophy and religion. And he would draw from all religions—maybe in order, wittingly or no, to make one of his own. He would synthesize. He would interpret imagery. He would examine myths. He would call upon coins, the stars, legends, rituals from tribes and peoples all over. For Miss O'Connor, the plain materialism of Freudianism was at least that—agnostics doing the best they could to learn about their heads, and in excessive moments, revealing how much they inadvertently craved certain (religious) consolations. But Jung and his followers were addressing themselves to the spiritual, and really telling one another (and others, through books and articles and lectures) that they had truths not only about the mind's life, but the soul's—a psychology of the soul. For Miss O'Connor such an approach was a transgression; a misunderstanding of what the soul is; and an exceptionally dangerous kind of pride. We all at moments show how thoughtless or arrogant we are; but relatively few decide that they are in a position to challenge the various religious faiths—to weigh and sift and in an ultimate sense of the word *judge* (with respect to the transcendent). A presumptuousness of Jung's matched only by the craven gullibility, Miss O'Connor knew, of his ardent followers, whose capacity to absorb and dote upon murkiness has to be remarked upon.

As one goes through the O'Connor correspondence the philosophical sophistication of her mind becomes apparent. Once when I was in Milledgeville I spent time looking at her books, examining some of her marginal notations. She had at her fingertips an impressive library—Aquinas and Maritain, Augustine and Teilhard de Chardin, Freud and Jung; but also Gilson, Bloy, Tillich, Romano Guardini, Eric Voegelin, and Gabriel Marcel. She had, too, the wisdom of novelists, Catholic and non-Catholic: Bernanos and Mauriac, Hawthorne and Melville, Tolstoy and Dostoievsky, Dickens and Eliot and Hardy. The following excerpt from one of her letters, by no means atypical, reveals what went through the mind of a woman who could, again, refer to intellectuals as "interleckchuls," and be scornful of much that has been taken to heart by important elements in contemporary American culture: "I am currently reading Etienne Gilson's *History of Christian Philosophy in the Middle Ages* and I am surprised to come across various answers to Simone Weil's questions to Fr. Perrin. St. Justin Martyr anticipated her in the 2nd century on the question of the Logos enlightening every man who comes into the world. This is really one of her central questions and St. Justin answered it in what I am sure would have been her own way. Gilson is a vigorous writer, more so than Maritain; the other thing I have read of his is *The Unity of Philosophical Experience*, which I am an admirer of."

We have there no anxious lecturer, choosing as a strategy of self-defense a vigorous offense: look what *I* know, or want you to think I know—lest any of you try to slip me up. Nor do we have an essayist doing likewise, or parading her erudition immodestly before her all too awed readers: the sins of one soul finding congenial amplification elsewhere. Rather, a friend is unselfconsciously offering ideas, abstruse one time, quite connected to everyday living the next. As soon as that just-quoted portion of the letter ends, we read this: "My being on the crutches is not an accident or the energy-depriving ailment either but something that has been coming on in the top of the leg bone, a softening of it on acct. of a failure of circulation to the hip."

Hers was a mind able to move back and forth with a certain ease between matters transcendent and matters immanent. Hers was a mind inquiring, discerning, analytic, yet appreciative of the mysterious, if not the mystical. She gave close attention to "local things," but she repeatedly entertained those larger conjectures about life in general. She was as delighted with a letter "from a West Virginia mountaineer whose favorite word is 'literature' which he spells 'litatur,'" as she was with letters from people she referred to as scholars. In one letter she was referring to Santayana or Kafka, in the next, she is telling a friend that she had "never read Kraft-Ebbing or *Memoirs of Hecate County*." To which comment she added, tersely: "A little self-knowledge goes a long way."

She had strong preferences, a decided notion of what her own taste is, and ought be. She said a lot when she said "I am a Catholic." She added a lot when she followed up those four words with the modification that she was "a Catholic peculiarly possessed by the modern consciousness." And she added a lot more when she noted this: "My audience are the people who think God is dead. At least these are the people I am conscious of writing for." And if anyone tried to update that God, as a way of making Him no longer dead for many of today's people, she could be contemptuously blunt: "As for Jesus' being a realist: if He was not God, He was no realist, only a liar, and the crucifixion an act of justice."

It is no small revelation to find her saying that Simone Weil and Edith Stein "are the two 20th century women who interest me most." They were, of course, two intellectual Jewesses who searched hard for God; one died coming closer, ever closer, to the Catholic Church, the other embraced it fully and ended up a nun. They were women who had to deal with their own strong intellects, tough and demanding wills; and they were women who moved an uncommon and unlikely distance—from sectarian intellectuality to a necessary surrender of the same to a higher authority, the Person of God, and in one instance, the Church that claims to hold continuing custody of His flesh and blood. Such a surrender, O'Connor knew, was enabled by grace. Born to Catholicism, she knew the believer's doubts. Despite her assertion that for her "dogma is only a gateway to contemplation and is an instrument of freedom and not of restriction," she could also, in the same letter, confess to a friend: "When I ask myself how I know I believe, I have no satisfactory answer at all, no assurance at all, no feeling at all. I can only say with Peter, Lord I believe, help my unbelief. And all I can say about my love of God is, Lord help me in my lack of it. I distrust pious phrases, particularly when they issue from my mouth."

Her freely admitted complicity with her readers, with respect to the polarity of religious belief and doubt, may help us comprehend the vehemence of her occasional attacks on a group known for its skepticism, the intelligentsia. Add to that problem a southerner's distrust of outsiders, especially preachy ones—as well as a sensitive southerner's appreciation of the moral case those outsiders had, however a matter of history, rather than of something earned—and one has, perhaps, all that is needed for an explanation of why a most learned woman could turn so sour when contemplating her own kind, many of whom, it has to be added, were also *not* her own kind in important respects. All she could do, she surely understood, was live out the contradictions within herself, and note those within a number of others. She pointedly affirmed, in a letter to an anonymous friend, this limited but significant connection to Hulga: "It's not said that she [Hulga] has never had any faith but it is implied that her fine education has got rid of it for her, that purity has been overridden by pride of intellect through her fine education."

She knew that the poor, the uneducated, can also be thoroughly impure, as wretched spiritually as the rest of us who are by far luckier. Did Christ promise *every* poor person admission to Heaven? A socioeconomic fact become an existential one! Each of us, rich or poor, holds on to the possibility of grace, holds on with one's teeth, if one is Flannery O'Connor. For her the loss of hope is a large sin, certainly. She had every intention as a writer of providing that hope, giving it the most palpable and suggestive form her wits as a storyteller enabled: "All my stories are about the action of grace on a character who is not very willing to support it, but most people think of these stories as hard, hopeless, brutal, etc." And to spell out what she meant about those people, she said this: "Part of the difficulty of all this is that you write for an audience who doesn't know what grace is and don't recognize it when they see it."

She was part of that audience, she knew. Who can assume he or she is not? She wrote out of a "terrible need," a phrase she once used in connection with a religious hunger she felt evident in her friend Katherine Anne Porter. She wrote in fear, too. It is hard for many intellectuals to understand this kind of intellectual, whose worries are indeed obsessive, in the nonpsychiatric and nonpejorative sense of the word; they are worries best indicated by an aphoristic phrase she once coined: "When there is nothing over the intellect it usually is tyrannical." She knew, Simone Weil knew, Edith Stein knew, the tyrannical side of a brilliantly aspiring philosophical mind, impatient with low-level discourse and outraged by the fake postures that others have no trouble calling upon for themselves. Tyrants lack charity—brilliant tyrants included. To feel charity is to have received grace. One senses Simone Weil, at the end, fighting hard against the imperial insistence of her own fiercely logical, perceptive, appraising mind. One senses Flannery O'Connor running to her southern country people, not because she saw them as saved—pure, righteous, God-fearing; she understood the southern scene too well for such an unqualified generalization. But she did find in that scene her particular refuge—a spiritual home as well as a place where she lived and died. Among people far less intellectual than herself she could, perhaps, keep the tyranny of her mind under greater control than would have been the case had she lived in places where that tyranny is rampant, even celebrated.

When she says that she believes "there is a fine grain of stupidity required in the fiction writer"; when she says that "the meaning in a story can't be paraphrased and if it's there it's there, almost more as a physical than an intellectual fact"; when she curtly declares that "subtlety is the curse of man"; when she talks of "sterile intellect"; when she announces that she's had "a stomach full of liberal religion"; when she talks of "a Unitarian or some pious liberal fraud," she is having a good time being scandalous, or she is being teasing and funny, or she is letting loose with a barb to friends who are, like her, themselves part of what is being criticized. But most of all she is fighting for her own respect. She knew how brilliant she was, and how successful she had ended up being. The word *celebrity* was used by her correspondents, and she could scarcely deny the fact that in a rather short writing career a great deal of attention had been given to her writing, and, inevitably these days, to her as a person. Such a secular triumph was, for a person of her sensibility, a mixed blessing. "You will have found Christ," she told a friend, "when you are concerned with other people's sufferings and not your own."

At the time (1961), not far from death herself and not unfamiliar with pain, she knew the extreme danger of what she once called a "swollen faith" in oneself: pride, self-centeredness, narcissism—the particular name or label meant little, the habit or attitude rather a lot. This continuing struggle with herself was the mark of her kind of intellectuality. I believe that it was a struggle enhanced both by her Catholicism and her life as a southerner. Anyone who has read Georges Bernanos, his polemical essays and his fiction, will recognize the struggle: a sensitive and thoughtful writer, a man of ideas—many, many of them—who turned with outbursts of vehement denunciation on his own kind. Like her he loved the poor, saw them as God's chosen people; and like her, he profoundly distrusted the intelligentsia, which he regarded as pagan and self-centered. At the same time, their vanity was his lifelong temptation—as an essayist, a storyteller, a person anxious to tell others what they ought think, like, dislike, do. And like her, he gave geographical expression to this profound torment: Paris, the place of sin, the city where all those editors and publishers and writers and artists and academics lived. Eventually, after wandering through his beloved France, he imposed exile on himself. From far-off Paraguay and Brazil he could be the *true* Frenchman—and rail against those who have corrupted what he wanted, a nation-state merged with a church into a pure community of believing, confessing Christians. The secular world constantly scandalized him—and unnervingly reminded him of his own pride. In desperation, he clung to his fiction and hoped through it to redeem himself and help a few others in their spiritual struggles.

It is not too hard, going through Flannery O'Connor's fiction and nonfiction, to find similar themes. Her cracks about New York, about Greenwich Village, about writers and publishers and magazines and colleges and, always, the intellectuals, are meant to show, by their repetition and their adroit aim, a sense of affiliation and a certain complicity with what is criticized—the former earned, the latter an inevitable consequence of the recognition she achieved. She could, too, direct her satire nearer home. "My mail for the last two weeks has been from rural Georgia," she told her good friend Maryat Lee in 1959; and after a recitation (which borders on the condescending) of the odd ones who wrote, she observes that "these letters are from people I might have made up. I don't want to get any nearer to them than in the imagination either." It is one of the least guarded comments to come from her, in a voluminous and forthright correspondence. She was often quick to chide fellow southerners who had left the region, such as Maryat Lee. And God help any Yankee who tried to give her a secular sermon of any kind. But here she was, acknowledging the nonsense and stupidity and arrogance and pettiness that are to be found, she always knew, in rural Georgia as well as the Sodom and Gommorah places up North. And here she was keeping her distance from what she disliked, and inevitably, judged—through humor and scorn.

A proper sense of her own nature, as an educated, reasonably well-to-do person, made such a reaction quite expectable. Who was she to like everyone, to deny her own life in an effort to reach out, indiscriminately, to the poor and the rich, the ignorant and the educated, the rural and the urban, the southern and the northern? She was no saint; she was a sinner. That simple and obvious statement was for her the most profound kind of psychological assessment—one that enables an understanding of her prejudices, her narrowness, her demanding schoolteacher's asides, her querulous moments. But if she sinned she also felt the continual scrutiny of a strenuous Christian conscience that was never tougher on anyone than with herself. She referred in late 1961 to "a grace which neither you [the correspondent] nor I nor Elizabeth Bishop [the poet] in the remotest sense possesses, but which Sister Evangelist, for example, does." Nor did she necessarily see that grace as only the property of nuns and priests: "It doesn't have to be associated with religion; I am just trying to isolate this kind of abandonment of self which is the result of sanctifying grace . . . faith is blindness and now you can see."

With that remark she got close indeed to the essence of what she was about as a writer—and as a person, one realizes, in the face of her extraordinary and compelling correspondence. Her characters, one after another, come to mind as one reads and reads again that section of a letter—especially the paradoxical comment worthy, surely, of Pascal's pensées: "Faith is blindness and now you can see." Hazel Motes, specifically and naturally; but also Tarwater, and Grandfather Head and his grandson Nelson, and those sad and lost ones, Julian or Hulga, who have not attained faith, for sure, but who have been visited with an "intervention" that impinges directly, severely, on their sense of self. It is an intervention that entails humiliation and loss; a subsequent erosion of that cocksure, moralizing inclination that Miss O'Connor knew better than to locate only north of the Mason and Dixon Line, or in the Taulkinhams of the South. And an intervention that sets the stage for a possible gain—the mind a bit cleaner, a bit less self-deluded.

All the time she was presenting us with versions of ourselves dressed up as grotesques located in a distant land—hence easier for us to look at. She knew her enemy—another kind of blindness than that connected to faith. She wanted to creep up on us, get us to notice not some rural Georgia freak, but our own desperation: freaks in Heaven's eye, freaks as Satan was known and felt to be. She did not really want to insult us or mock us. An artist, she used what she had—a gift of narrative, the ability to laugh at the world's small and big fish and the ability to make us do likewise. Some of her critics have lamented that she leaves the reader no sanctuary, no person, place or thing to regard as reassuring, as worthy of giving one's respect and affection to. Hazel Motes may be edging toward Heaven, but he is hardly one for many of us to emulate or admire. Similarly with Tarwater or Julian or Asbury or the mothers of the last two or Parker or his wife. And that is the way Miss O'Connor was determined to have it. She knew that many of her readers craved not grace but "role-models" and "social techniques" and "people to admire most"—or on a higher level, heroes to emulate; and if they could be called "existential heroes," then how wonderful, how thrilling, how fascinating: a Prometheus, here and there, for our time.

Her eyes, however, were on the lookout for something else—for God's terrible mercy. She was not a Greek dramatist or a Roman narrator. She was not a political essayist turned novelist or a sociologist with a literary flair. She had no great interest in probing minds or setting down a chronicle of sexual acrobatics. She didn't really care whether we left her novels with a "figure" we could "identify with." She knew she could hook us; she was a very good writer. But she wanted to do more than hold us spellbound. She wanted us to leave her words laughing and questioning. Laughing with her, but also at ourselves; and questioning not the meaning (within meaning, within meaning) of her stories, but, again, ourselves: what do we believe in, apart from all the blandishments offered us in this best of worlds, and where are we headed—other than to the suburbs, or a psychiatrist's office, or the Rotary, or the stacks in the campus library, and on and on? She wanted to emphasize the scandal of our lives, not the psychopathology or the social malaise or the cultural impasse of one kind or another. She wanted us to get the greatest possible distance on ourselves, hence her refusal to let us dig in and find ourselves yet another bit of solace: a Flannery O'Connor character who reassures us and tells us how good we are, because we are "like" him or her.

She was, all her life, "waiting for God"—Pascal's expression, Simone Weil's. She admired them both as proud and wonderfully gifted intellectuals who knew how hard it is for anyone, certainly including themselves, to attain—to be graced by—what she called an abandonment of self. To that end she worked hard as a writer; many of her characters did indeed feel themselves much diminished. And no wonder the crisis of confusion and outrage from many of us: why should anyone, these days, dare peddle *that*? We want heightening, enlargement, buoying up—consciousness expansion, ego support, actualization. Not from her that stuff; she would as soon have thrown away her beloved old typewriter than give us a polished up version of what so many of us have come to expect from each other during this, our second or two of earthly life.

She sat there in Baldwin County, Georgia, dying, burning with life, praying, reading, pouring out her soul's worries, reservations, deepest yearnings. She wrote for herself, for those she knew and loved, for any of us who cares to stop and look and listen. She wrote in the wish that she, that her readers, might be granted a moment or longer of surcease from ourselves, that we might transcend what we're called or considered, a Yankee this or a southern that, and instead become the property of Another, of Someone who long ago indicated His impatience with the various categorizations we use to put people in various places. She was herself a southern intellectual, a writer with few peers in the recent American past, and a writer, also, of enormous promise, taken from us far too soon. But finally, one believes, she was a soul blinded by faith; hence with an uncanny endowment of sight. She had a large smile. She had the generosity of one who wanted company along a tough but extremely important journey; and she was willing to work hard as a writer to earn the attentive regard of that company.

REFERENCES

THE CRITICAL RESPONSE to Flannery O'Connor's stories, novels, essays has grown steadily in the fifteen years since her death and shows no sign of abating. Her correspondence, published in 1979, will surely give further encouragement to those of us who continue to find her literary and spiritual voyage exceptional. I don't pretend as a reader to have exhausted the O'Connor critical canon, but over the years I've been reading with great interest the books and essays stimulated by her writing, and I want to mention what I have read and rather often found extremely helpful.

A volume that has weathered well is *The Added Dimension: The Art and Mind of Flannery O'Connor*, a collection of fine essays edited by Melvin J. Friedman and Lewis A. Lawson (New York: Fordham University Press, 1966). The latter editor has included an extraordinarily inclusive bibliography—O'Connor's writing and that of her critics. Those readers who have immersed themselves in the critical literature devoted to Walker Percy will recognize Mr. Lawson as a spiritual comrade of both those novelists, and a valuable host of sorts to the body of exegetical work that has followed publication of their fiction. An essay of Mr. Friedman's in this book is used again in a valuable book he has edited on Catholic novelists of the twentieth century: *The Vision Obscured* (New York: Fordham University Press, 1970).

In 1969 Carter Martin published *The True Country* (Nashville: Vanderbilt University Press), which examined certain "themes in the fiction of Flannery O'Connor." The book made a strong case for the Catholic orthodoxy that runs through stories apparently and paradoxically concerned with the predominantly anti-Catholic south Georgia precincts of the Bible Belt. An altogether different—startlingly so—mode of interpretation was offered the next year by Josephine Hendin in *The World of Flannery O'Connor* (Bloomington: Indiana University Press, 1970). Ms. Hendin's approach is distinctly at variance with the heavily theological and philosophical line of inquiry pursued by most other critics. She is a psychologically sensitive reader, willing at times to connect the mental life she spots and analyzes in O'Connor's fiction to the author's personal life and that of her mother. The comic side of O'Connor's writing is down-played in favor of the serious, even psychopathological elements which, of course, attracted the attention of many of us, destined, if not doomed, to live in a century so stuck on itself for its psychological "awareness." I was made uncomfortable by Ms. Hendin, as I have not been by any other O'Connor critic. Perhaps a degree of blindness was made apparent. Perhaps some "defensiveness" was brought to consciousness. Or maybe the jarring effect of two writers from two different worlds, nevertheless coming into stark contact, serves to keep one's nerves on edge.

A more conventionally theological approach appeared in *The Eternal Crossroads*, an examination of "the art of Flannery O'Connor" by Leon V. Driskell and Joan T. Brittain (Lexington: University of Kentucky Press, 1971). The authors are good at analyzing the important influence of Pierre Teilhard de Chardin on O'Connor. And further exploration in the same direction came out the next year: *The Christian Humanism of Flannery O'Connor*, by David Eggenschwiler (Detroit: Wayne State University Press, 1972). Similarly suffused with Christian sensibility is Sister Kathleen Feeley's *Flannery O'Connor: Voice of the Peacock* (New Brunswick: Rutgers University Press, 1972). There is a brief but important and suggestive introduction by Caroline Gordon, for so long a mentor to Miss O'Connor. And in Miles Orvell's quite strong and valuable *Invisible Parade* (Philadelphia: Temple University Press, 1972), I have found shrewd, restrained, thoughtful interpretations of O'Connor's fiction. He obviously admires and *loves* her stories and two novels. Yet he possesses a distance on her work and the region she lived in—a distance I certainly can't lay claim to. His line-by-line reading of her writing is close, yet gracefully unpedantic.

More recently we have Martha Stephens' *The Question of Flannery O'Connor* (Baton Rouge: Louisiana State University Press, 1973), a strong, appreciative yet critical look at the fiction, with some good bibliographical suggestions; and Preston M. Browning's *Flannery O'Connor* (Carbondale: Southern Illinois University Press, 1974), which provides a general survey of her life and work. Mention should also be made of two extremely helpful monographs, both published a bit earlier, in Stanley Edgar Hyman's wonderfully appreciative and at times lyrical *Flannery O'Connor* (Minneapolis: University of Minnesota Press, 1966) and Robert Drake's religiously informed essay, "Flannery O'Connor" (Grand Rapids, Mich.: William B. Eremans, 1966).

Since 1972 Georgia College at Milledgeville has issued *The Flannery O'Connor Bulletin*, six issues to date, each with interesting critical essays. At Georgia State one can "visit with" her library, come a bit closer to her spirit. One can, in nearby Milledgeville, in the drugstores, at the gas stations, catch a glimpse, an earful of what she started out with—on her fictional and religious way, so to speak. A Holiday Inn may be across the street from the O'Connor farm, Andalusia, but once one walks down the path of that country place, O'Connor's South comes into view. I recommend, too, a trip to Savannah. The sight of Flannery O'Connor's particular, early childhood, "southern scene"—a home on one of that city's marvelous squares, under the shadow of its imposing Catholic cathedral—is about all (one prays) any of this century's ambitious "psycho-historians" would need to understand the early "influences" upon her mind, her soul.

I want to mention, again, Robert Fitzgerald's splendid essay "The Countryside and the True Country," an important interpretative piece, *Sewanee Review*, LXX (Summer, 1962). He knows what she was struggling for—and against. His essay I quoted with respect to anti-intellectualism was titled "Bejeweled: The Great Sun," a review of the thinking of another great American anti-intellectual, William Carlos Williams (*New Republic*, April 25, 1949).

In the quarterlies, there are so many fine essays devoted to Miss O'Connor's life or work; I only mention here three that for my wife and me have special importance: "Flannery O'Connor's Devil," by John Hawkes, *Sewanee Review*, LXX (Summer, 1962); "Flannery O'Connor's Campaign for Her Country," an obituary and touching appreciation, by Brainard Cheney, *Sewanee Review*, LXXII (Autumn, 1964); and nearer to our time, Marion Montgomery's first-rate "Flannery O'Connor and the Jansenist Problem in Fiction," *Southern Review*, XIV (Summer, 1978).

And finally, I came across two books in 1978 that I thought the wide-ranging yet insistently, toughly, unashamedly circumscribed sensibility of Flannery O'Connor might have appreciated, had she been given leave to remain longer with us: Harry Crews's *A Childhood*, his biography of a place (New York: Harper and Row, 1978). The place is Bacon County, Georgia, not all that far from Baldwin County—a kin county in many respects. Crews did not grow up a well-to-do Georgian as O'Connor did; he is, it can be argued, one of her country characters become, ironically (and heroically), a writer, a novelist. The terror and violence—but also the moments of attempted, if flawed, honor and decency—are his to relate personally and were hers to see and evoke with astonishing delicacy, accuracy, success. I also refer to a splendid, and splendidly produced, book by an art historian (Anita Schorsch) and a biblical scholar (Martin Greif) titled *The Morning Stars Sang: The Bible in Popular and Folk Art* (New York: Main Street Press, 1978). This beautifully written and illustrated book attempts to do justice to the religious spirit of thousands of "ordinary" men and women—a spirit that engaged, time and again, with art in many, diverse, and altogether wondrous ways. Popular and folk art devoted to the Bible, efforts to render its stories, once more, in a version that reaches, moves, inspires—they make up the stuff of this book. They are efforts that a rather extraordinary artist of words, plots, and character portrayals would have found welcome, gratifying, and morally on the right track.